How to do a Systematic Literature Review in Nursing

Literature Review in Nursing

A step-by-step guide

How to do a Systematic Literature Review in Nursing

A step-by-step guide

Josette Bettany-Saltikov

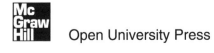
Open University Press

Open University Press
McGraw-Hill Education
McGraw-Hill House
Shoppenhangers Road
Maidenhead
Berkshire
England
SL6 2QL

email: enquiries@openup.co.uk
world wide web: www.openup.co.uk

and Two Penn Plaza, New York, NY 10121-2289, USA

First published 2012

A catalogue record of this book is available from the British Library

ISBN-13: 978-0-33-524227-6
ISBN-10: 0-33-524227-8
eISBN: 978-0-33-524228-3

Library of Congress Cataloging-in-Publication Data
CIP data applied for

Typesetting and e-book compilations by
RefineCatch Limited, Bungay, Suffolk
Printed and bound by CPI Group (UK) Ltd, Croydon, CRO 4YY

Fictitious names of companies, products, people, characters and/or data that may
be used herein (in case studies or in examples) are not intended to represent any
real individual, company, product or event.

The **McGraw·Hill** Companies

Contents

List of boxes

List of figures

List of tables

Foreword

In today's society the nurse faces ongoing and continuous challenges related to the advancement of medicine, technology and nursing practice, in addition to the effects of a global economic downturn. A continuous challenge for the profession is the need to underpin nursing practice on the best available evidence. The need for research-based nursing has been high on the agenda for policy makers in the UK for at least two decades; more recently replaced by the broader notion of evidence based nursing (EBN). In addition to research evidence, evidence based nursing includes the use of other available evidence such as clinical judgement, expert opinion and experience (McSherry *et al.* 2006).

Considerable discussion emerges within the literature with regard to the extent to which nursing practice is actually based upon the best available evidence (Strange 2001). Reasons for this include attitudes of staff to EBN, knowledge and skill levels, availability of evidence and support for staff in the clinical area. Although nurses' attitudes towards using evidence are mostly reported as positive, they often find reading and analyzing research a challenge. Reasons for this include the way the research is written and the jargon associated with it, as well as the level of support received. Previous studies over numbers of years have found that the attitudes of nursing staff to using evidence were consistently positive (McSherry *et al.* 2006). However barriers that exist within the clinical area include the nurses own knowledge and skill, time constraints and in particular the support and encouragement received within the clinical area (Bradshaw 2010; Parahoo 2000).

However, Bettany-Saltikov's book offers great hope in this regard. Written in a nice, easy to read style, the author demystifies both the reading and understanding of research. Through the engaging style used in the book, nurses are encouraged to engage with the research literature and perform a literature review. Whether doing this as part of a course or to improve practice, all the required tools and skills are clearly explained within this text.

Bettany-Saltikov starts quite sensibly by asking the reader to focus on the research question or the problem in practice, and then takes them logically through the steps of narrowing down the topic and searching the literature. Use of the PICO framework is a very useful suggestion and common research approaches found in the literature are clearly explained. Being able to critically appraise research is a key skill required by registered nurses. This is comprehensively covered within the book, with useful templates and tips to help the readers' developing knowledge. The book is also supported by useful and practical case scenarios.

Now more than ever it is essential that nurses ensure their care is evidence based. We are encouraged to find ways to 'engage staff nurses' in the ENB 'movement' (Bradshaw 2010). Bettany-Saltikov is likely to contribute to this movement in a big way. This lively and engaging book takes the mystery out of reading, analyzing and reviewing the literature in a way which will encourage current and forthcoming practitioners to develop the key skills required for EBN. Having taught this subject for a number of years, this is certainly one of the best books I have seen on the topic. It will be hard to keep on the shelves!

Prof. Fiona Timmins
Associate Professor
School of Nursing and Midwifery
Trinity College Dublin

References

Bradshaw, W.G. (2010) Importance of nursing leadership in advancing evidence-based nursing practice, *Neonatal Network*, vol. 29, no. 2, pp. 117–122.

Gerrish, K. and Clayton, J. (2004) Promoting evidence-based practice: an organizational approach, *Journal of Nursing Management*, vol. 12, pp. 114–123.

McSherry, R., Artley, A. and Halloran, J. (2006) Research Awareness: An Important Factor for Evidence-Based Practice? *World Views on Evidence Based Nursing*, vol. 3, no. 3, pp. 103–115.

Parahoo, K. (2000) Barriers to, and facilitators of research utilization among nurses in Northern Ireland, *Journal of Advanced Nursing*, vol. 31, no. 1, pp. 89–98.

Strange, F. (2001) The persistence of ritual in nursing practice, *Clinical Effectiveness in Nursing*, vol. 5, no. 4, pp. 177–183.

Acknowledgements

I would like to thank Mrs. Susan Hulme, Staff Nurse, Haematology Unit, North Tees Hospital, UK for her kind permission to re-use extracts from her BSc dissertation.

Thanks are also expressed to Dr. Robert McSherry who was the author of Chapter 9, 'Sharing, disseminating and using systematic reviews to inform and improve nursing practice'. Dr. McSherry is Professor of Nursing and Practice Development at Teesside University. He has recently completed a full-time secondment (March–July 2011) as Deputy Director of Nursing/Professor of Nursing and Practice Development with Mid Staffordshire National Health Service Foundation Trust. Rob also completed a part-time secondment (October 2009–September 2010) with the North East Strategic Health Authority as a Senior Nurse Advisor and was appointed Clinical Associate Professor with the Australian Catholic University, Brisbane Australia (March 2007–March 2010). Rob's work has focused on promoting patient safety, people-centred care, and quality nursing, and his main aim is seeing research being used at a frontline clinical level, at which nurses and other health professionals are equipped with the essential skills and knowledge to aid with the delivery of evidence-based practice. Rob has shared and disseminated his work around practice development, healthcare governance, and evidence-informed practice internationally through publications, conferences, consultancy, and workshops.

Introduction

'I have been told I need to undertake a systematic literature review! Where do I start?' Many people may have been told this by their supervisors, directors, managers or consultants and shared this same reaction. Conducting a systematic literature review is one of the activities you may need to carry out whether you are writing your dissertation for an undergraduate nursing degree, fulfilling the requirements for a master's degree, undertaking continuing professional development or simply answering a clinical question from practice.

This book is intended for nurses in practice, nursing students, nurse lecturers teaching at universities and other healthcare professionals in a diverse range of settings. The book provides a simple step-by-step approach to conducting a systematic literature review. I have tried to present all the content in this book in a simple and clear format in order to make it suitable for all levels of learning from BSc upwards.

A conversational style has been used to engage the reader, as I know from first-hand experience that many students are put off research if the content is presented in a very academic way and full of jargon. My view is that a systematic literature review is not just for doctors or high-level Cochrane Review researchers. Anyone with basic undergraduate research skills is capable of undertaking this type of review. I can say this confidently because I have taught this method of reviewing to hundreds of nursing students over more than seven years.

When I taught a systematic literature review module and the term 'systematic review' was mentioned, many students started panicking and said, 'I don't know how to do this!' But my experience on a number of dissertation modules has shown that once the individual steps are explained in a straightforward manner, all students, including undergraduate nurses, master's students, mature returning nurses and nurse practitioners, are capable of undertaking a complete systematic review to a high standard.

This is a practical book that you can use when conducting your own systematic review. Many examples, activities, case studies and templates have been provided to enable you to undertake each part of the review process with confidence. The chapters discuss every step from the beginning to the end of the systematic review. The following is an overview of the book's chapters.

Chapter 1: What is a systematic review?

This chapter introduces the term 'systematic review' and discusses the purpose and different types of systematic reviews and common databases for finding these reviews. The chapter describes their role within evidence-based nursing practice, the differences between literature (narrative) reviews and systematic reviews, and the medical hierarchy of evidence. The chapter concludes by discussing the drawbacks and limitations of systematic reviews.

Chapter 2: Asking an answerable and focused review question

This chapter lists the key points to remember when selecting a review topic and describes the different ways of narrowing the review topic to a specific question. The chapter discusses the meaning and functions of an answerable and focused review question, and the main types of focused research questions. The chapter provides some examples from nursing practice. This is followed by a presentation on the different types of research questions and the importance of selecting the appropriate research design for the type of research question you have selected. The chapter provides a number of templates to help you formulate your own answerable and focused review question.

Chapter 3: Writing the plan and background to your review

This chapter describes the key factors that need to be considered when writing a plan (or protocol) for your systematic literature review. The chapter describes the different sections within the plan and provides examples. The first stage of the plan, the background, is discussed in detail and excerpts included to clarify this process. (In-depth details for each stage of the rest of the plan and review are provided in the ensuing chapters.) This chapter suggests different tools to help you start writing the background for your own review plan.

Chapter 4: Specifying your objectives and inclusion and exclusion criteria

This chapter discusses the meanings and differences between a problem statement, a review question, aims and objectives. The chapter discusses methods for specifying the inclusion and exclusion criteria and provides examples for different quantitative and qualitative review questions. The chapter provides templates to help you write out your own problem statement, aims and objectives as well as your inclusion and exclusion criteria.

Chapter 5: Conducting a comprehensive and systematic literature search

This chapter considers the importance, rationale and the aims of undertaking a comprehensive and systematic search. The chapter describes the key factors to be considered when undertaking a comprehensive search and the steps involved in converting your review question into a comprehensive search strategy.

Chapter 6: Working with your primary papers: selecting, appraising and extracting data

This chapter lists the main stages involved in working with your primary research papers. The first stage includes ways of selecting appropriate papers to answer your review question. This stage is conducted in two parts. First, you select your papers based on the title and abstract according to your predetermined criteria. Second, you repeat this process when reading the full paper. The next stage involves appraising the quality of your primary research papers that you have selected by using standardized quality evaluation frameworks. Finally, ways of extracting the appropriate qualitative and quantitative data from your research papers are discussed. The chapter clarifies the importance of making or using a form or framework to standardize and increase the reliability and validity for all stages of the process by using relevant examples from nursing practice.

Chapter 7: Synthesizing, summarizing and presenting your findings

This chapter describes the issues that you need to consider when summarizing, synthesizing and presenting the results of your quantitative or qualitative systematic literature review in nursing practice. A narrative synthesis needs to be included for whatever type of data you have extracted. This can be done by using a number of different tools to summarize, organize and condense your data. Do remember that the results of all the methods you have undertaken within your review need to be presented. A key point when summarizing, synthesizing and presenting your results is to make sure that you present everything in a clear, transparent and easy to understand format.

Chapter 8: Writing up your discussion and completing your review

This chapter discusses ways of structuring the 'discussion section' of your systematic literature review. The chapter presents extracts from case studies and a completed systematic review. The chapter provides suggestions for writing up your review report and tips for improving academic writing skills.

Chapter 9: Sharing, disseminating and using systematic reviews to inform and improve nursing practice

This chapter describes the importance of sharing and disseminating the findings. The chapter defines the terms 'sharing' and 'disseminating' and highlights their relevance to spreading the findings from systematic reviews. The chapter illustrates practical tips and ways of sharing and disseminating systematic reviews and considers some of the models and frameworks to enable and support innovation and change in organizations providing nursing practice. The chapter outlines enabling and inhibiting factors associated with the implementation of the findings of systematic reviews in practice.

1 What is a systematic review?

Overview

- What is a systematic review?
- What is the purpose of systematic reviews within nursing practice?
- What is the role of systematic reviews within evidence-based nursing practice?
- What is the difference between a literature (narrative) review and a systematic review?
- Where can systematic reviews be found?
- What are the drawbacks and limitations of systematic reviews?

What is a systematic review?

A systematic review is a summary of the research literature that is focused on a single question. It is conducted in a manner that tries to identify, select, appraise and synthesize all high quality research evidence relevant to that question. High quality research includes those studies with an explicit and rigorous design that allow the findings to be interrogated against clear contexts and research intentions. When conducting systematic reviews, we need to accept that there is a hierarchy of evidence and that what can confidently be stated *empirically* about the world is derived from studies where the design is both explicit and rigorous. Distinctions are therefore made between 'evidence' and 'experience'. The first has been rigorously obtained and scrutinized, the latter has simply been noted, organized and reported. An understanding of systematic reviews and how to implement them in practice is now becoming mandatory for all nurses and other healthcare professionals (Centre for Evidence-Based Medicine 2009).

What is the purpose of systematic reviews within nursing practice?

The Centre for Reviews and Dissemination (University of York) states:

> Healthcare decisions for individual patients and for public policy should be informed by the best available research evidence. Practitioners and decision-makers are encouraged to make use of the latest research and information about best practice, and to ensure that decisions are demonstrably rooted in this knowledge.
>
> (Centre for Reviews and Dissemination 2008: v)

Following this advice can sometimes be difficult for nurse practitioners and researchers because of the large amount of information published in a multitude of journals world-wide. Individual research studies may be *biased* or methodologically unsound and can reach conflicting conclusions. Examples of conflicting research results are frequently found in the media, which may announce that based on the research results of the latest study, the contraceptive pill is 'safe', and then a week later proclaim the exact opposite based on the results of another research study. In such situations it is not always clear which results are the most reliable, or which should be used as the basis of policy and practice decisions (Petticrew and Roberts 2006).

A systematic review should also be based on a peer review protocol (or plan) so that it can be easily replicated if necessary. The review itself will include a 'background' or introduction, in which the authors explain the scientific background or context to their study. It also includes the rationale for the systematic review indicating why it is necessary. The specific objectives and a summary of how the reviewer defined the criteria by which to choose the research papers are stated. Once a thorough assessment of the quality of each included research paper or report is carried out, all the individual studies are synthesized in an unbiased way. The findings are then interpreted and presented in an objective and independent summary (Hemmingway and Brereton 2009).

Systematic reviews are used by a wide diversity of professional and non-professional groups, including not only doctors, nurses and other healthcare professionals but also service users, policy makers, researchers, lecturers and students who want to keep up with the sometimes overwhelming amount of evidence in their field. It is important that nurses have the research skills to both understand and undertake systematic reviews, because they may want to know the answer to a clinical or research question or they may be conducting a systematic review in a dissertation required to complete a degree or as a continuing professional development requirement. Conducting a systematic review can initially appear to be an epic task, but once the steps of the process are learnt, and provided enough time is set aside, the task is relatively straightforward.

Having taught over 800 students on how to conduct this type of review on dissertation modules, I am confident that both undergraduate and postgraduate students can competently undertake and complete this type of review to a satisfactory level. If this is the first time you are undertaking this type of review, ensure that you carry it out in small steps and allow sufficient time to work on all the stages of the systematic review. It is important to understand that systematic reviews can be undertaken only on primary research papers. It is not possible to conduct a systematic review using other types of studies such as narrative reviews or opinion papers.

The three main types of systematic reviews are quantitative, qualitative and mixed method. Quantitative systematic reviews include only quantitative primary research studies while qualitative systematic reviews include only qualitative primary research studies. Mixed method reviews are based on both qualitative and quantitative studies; they are becoming more common nowadays, though they may be a bit more difficult to conduct. For the purposes of simplicity, this book will consider only the quantitative and qualitative types of reviews.

One of the best known sources for finding quantitative systematic reviews is the Cochrane Library, which concentrates mainly on synthesizing the findings of randomized controlled trials (RCTs). There is also a qualitative Cochrane Review database and the Campbell Collaboration database, where numerous qualitative systematic reviews can be found. Many systematic reviews are also published in key professional nursing journals.

What is the role of systematic reviews within evidence-based nursing practice?

The popularity of evidence-based practice has increased significantly since the mid-1990s, when Sackett et al. (1997) first coined the term. DiCenso et al. (1998) comment:

> In practising evidence-based nursing, a nurse has to decide whether the evidence is relevant for the particular patient. The incorporation of clinical expertise should be balanced with the risks and benefits of alternative treatments for each patient and should take into account the patient's unique clinical circumstances including comorbid conditions and preferences.
>
> (DiCenso et al. 1998: 38)

It is important to think about what is meant by the *best* research evidence. Within evidence-based practice there is a hierarchy of research evidence relating to studies with different types of research designs. This hierarchy has systematic reviews at the top and qualitative studies and opinion papers towards the bottom (Table 1.1). The

Table 1.1 Levels of evidence for different types of research questions

Level 1a	A well-conducted systematic review of randomized controlled trials
Level 1b	One good quality RCT
Level 1c	All or none studies
Level 2a	Systematic review of cohort studies
Level 2b	One cohort study
Level 2c	Outcomes research, i.e. the effect of an intervention or treatment
Level 3a	Systematic review of case control studies
Level 3b	Case series
Level 4	One case study
Level 5	Qualitative studies and expert opinion

Note: The research questions can include therapy, prevention, aetiology (causes) or harm.

hierarchy of evidence is a medically-based model which is considered by some professional groups to be biased towards quantitative research and intervention studies. Although qualitative studies are found at the bottom, it is important to consider that they answer very different types of questions relating to patient experiences. A number of authors and researchers have objected to the classification in Table 1.1, stating that this model does not accurately represent the high quality, qualitative research studies that inform policy and practice and which perhaps better represent patient experiences and preferences.

The traditional scientific approach to finding the best research evidence is to carry out or read a literature review (conducted by an expert or well-known figure in the field). However, these traditional (or narrative) reviews, even those written by experts,

> can be made to tell any story one wants them to and failure by literature reviewers to apply scientific principles to the process of reviewing, just as one would to primary research, can lead to biased conclusions, harm to patients and wasted resources.
>
> (Petticrew and Roberts 2006: 5)

Craig and Smyth (2007: 185) state: 'Because systematic reviews include a comprehensive search strategy, appraisal and synthesis of research evidence, they can be used as shortcuts in the evidence-based process'. Systematic reviews provide practitioners with a way of gaining access to predigested evidence. According to Petticrew and Roberts (2006: 9), systematic reviews 'adhere closely to a set of scientific methods that explicitly aim to limit systematic error (bias), mainly attempting to identify, appraise and synthesize all relevant studies (of whatever design) in order *to answer a particular question (or set of questions)*' (my emphasis). Systematic reviews substantially reduce the time and expertise it would take to locate, appraise and synthesize individual studies.

What is the difference between a literature (narrative) review and a systematic review?

Traditional literature (narrative) reviews can, as already mentioned, tell any story that the reviewer wants them to (Glasziou et al. 2001). For example, if the reviewer is a strong believer in the effectiveness of aspirin for treating headaches but does not believe that any other medication is effective, this reviewer could (hypothetically) select all the papers showing the effectiveness of aspirin and leave out all the ones showing the effectiveness of, say, ibuprofen.

While both traditional (narrative) and systematic reviews provide summaries of the available literature on a topic, they fulfil very different needs. Although narrative reviews (also called critical reviews) provide valuable summaries by experts on a wide topic area, they usually present an *overview*. These types of reviews do not usually follow a scientific review methodology and the papers included can be haphazard and biased. Nevertheless, they can be an important source of ideas, arguments, context and information. Narrative reviews are valuable because they are written by experts in the field and provide a general summary of the topic area, but they may not always include all the literature on the topic and sometimes they may be biased in terms of which articles are selected and discussed (Petticrew and Roberts 2006).

Narrative reviewers can be influenced by their preferred theories, needs and beliefs. It is important to remember that narrative reviews are usually driven by a general interest in a topic and *not* directed by a stated question. Narrative reviews do not state the criteria that determine the search undertaken and can be disorganized. A notorious example is the review conducted by the eminent doctor, Linus Pauling (1974), who was a Nobel prize laureate. In 1974, having conducted a non-systematic traditional review, he concluded that people should be getting 100 times the amount of vitamin C that the food and nutrition board recommended at the time; he suggested that such doses could *prevent* a cold. Some 30 years later Douglas et al. (2004) conducted a thorough systematic review of papers from the same period as Pauling's review; they concluded that high doses of vitamin C *did not prevent* colds (although this could reduce the duration by one or two days). Douglas et al. (2004) found that Pauling had failed to include 15 relevant studies in his review. It is therefore important to remember that 'a haphazard review, even one carried out by an expert, can be misleading' (Petticrew and Roberts 2006: 6).

A systematic review in contrast uses *a rigorous research methodology* to try to limit bias in all aspects of the review. In this sense it is close to a primary research study, where the participants are not people but rather the papers included in the review. Khan et al. (2003: 1) suggest that 'a systematic review is a research article that identifies relevant studies, appraises their quality and summarizes their results using a scientific methodology'. Table 1.2 summarizes the differences and similarities between the two types of reviews.

Table 1.2   Similarities and differences between a narrative review and a systematic review

	Systematic reviews	*Narrative reviews*
Question	Focused on a single question	Not necessarily focused on a single question but may describe an overview of a topic
Protocol	A peer review protocol (or plan) is included	No protocol
Background/literature review	Both provide summaries of the available literature on a topic	
Objectives	Has clear objectives stated	Objectives may or may not be identified
Inclusion/exclusion criteria	Criteria stated before the review is conducted	Criteria not usually specified
Search strategy	Comprehensive search conducted in a systematic way	Strategy not explicitly stated
Process of selecting papers	Selection process usually clear and explicit	Selection process not described
Process of evaluating papers	Comprehensive evaluation of study quality	Evaluation of study quality may or may not be included

(*continued overleaf*)

Table 1.2 Continued

	Systematic reviews	Narrative reviews
Process of extracting relevant information	Process is usually clear and specific	Process of extracting relevant information is not explicit and clear
Results/data synthesis	Clear summaries of studies based on high-quality evidence	Summary based on studies where the quality of included papers may not be specified, and can be influenced by reviewers' pet theories, needs and beliefs
Discussion	Written by an expert or group of experts with a detailed and well-grounded knowledge of the issues	

Where can systematic reviews be found?

Systematic reviews can be found in a number of different nursing journals and specialist websites. Box 1.1 provides some useful websites to start searching for systematic reviews.

Box 1.1 Websites for finding systematic reviews

- Evidence-Based Nursing (EBN)
  http://ebn.bmj.com
- TRIP Database
  www.tripdatabase.com
- Evidence in Health and Social Care
  www.nelh.nhs.uk
- Centre for Reviews and Dissemination (University of York)
  www.york.ac.uk/inst/crd
- Campbell Collaboration
  www.campbellcollaboration.org
- Cochrane Library
  www.thecochranelibrary.com
- Cochrane Qualitative Research Methods Group
  www.cqrmg.cochrane.org

What are the drawbacks and limitations of systematic reviews?

Although systematic reviews can be found at the top of the hierarchy of evidence, this does not mean that we should always believe the results presented within them. Like any other piece of research, a systematic review can be conducted badly, so it is important to have the skills to be able to appraise them (see Chapter 6). Systematic reviews may also be biased in the way they select their papers, for instance if they have not included all the primary research papers available. Sometimes systematic reviews include only English language papers and ignore all non-English language papers, which may have found different results

Other types of biases can occur in the way that reviewers search for their research papers. If the reviewers did not conduct a comprehensive search drawing on the most relevant databases, searching for grey literature and hand searching, it is possible that a number of key papers may have been left out. Further systematic reviews may not have properly combined the results of different studies appropriately and so ended up presenting inaccurate results.

It is crucial to appraise a systematic review properly before using the results. To do this you need to ask a series of questions to evaluate if the review in question conducted all the steps in the process correctly and with minimal bias.

Key points

- A systematic review is a research article that identifies a specific review question, identifies all relevant studies, appraises their quality and summarizes their results using a scientific methodology.
- It is possible to conduct systematic reviews of many different types of primary research studies.
- Sources for finding systematic reviews include the Cochrane Library, Campbell Collaboration, the Cochrane Qualitative Research Group and key nursing journals, among others.
- Systematic reviews are based on research evidence and the synthesis of research studies and can also be used to inform important policies that affect both the quality as well as the safety and value of healthcare.
- Because systematic reviews include a comprehensive search strategy, appraisal and synthesis of research evidence, they can be used as shortcuts in the evidence-based process.
- Both the traditional (narrative) and systematic reviews provide summaries of the available literature on a topic but fulfil very different needs.
- Narrative reviews provide valuable summaries by experts on a wide topic area and they usually present an *overview*.
- Narrative reviews do not follow a scientific review methodology and the papers included within them can be haphazard and biased, usually through the opinion of the study authors.

Summary

This chapter introduced the term 'systematic review' and discussed the purpose of these types of reviews within nursing research and practice. The chapter discussed different types of systematic reviews and common databases for finding them. Their role within evidence-based nursing practice and the differences between literature (narrative) reviews and systematic reviews were debated and the medical hierarchy of evidence briefly discussed. The chapter concluded by discussing the drawbacks and limitations of systematic reviews.

2 Asking an answerable and focused review question

Overview

- Selecting a topic area for your systematic review
- Narrowing the topic area to a specific answerable review question
- Using background or foreground questions: what is the difference?
- Factors to consider when asking answerable and focused review questions
- Developing your review question further
- Relating your question to the research design: what types of study designs should you look for to answer your research question?

Selecting a topic area for your systematic review

Selecting a topic area for your systematic review is the first step towards undertaking the review. The specific topic you select may arise from a number of different triggers. If you are a nursing student, your interest in a topic may result from a lecture or module on a medical condition that was covered in your undergraduate classes or a medical problem that you or a relative have experienced. The topic area may also arise from a contemporary issue highlighted in the media, such as reports on the latest research studies conducted on breast cancer or swine flu, or the measles, mumps and rubella (MMR) vaccine. If you are a practising nurse, it is likely that the topic area you choose is related to your professional practice or a Nursing and Midwifery Council issue or national initiative. Whatever your role, it is important that when selecting a research topic you bear in mind a number of key points (Box 2.1).

Box 2.1   Key points to remember when choosing a research topic

---

When choosing a research topic, you will need to identify:

- an area you are interested in related to your practice
- a question that you would like to know the answer to
- why the question is interesting and worth investigating
- issues relating to the question
- what you will gain by investigating the question
- what your profession and other professions will gain
- the rationale for asking the question
- the use of having the answer, i.e. ask 'So what?'
- the lack of knowledge in the area.

Narrowing the topic area to a specific answerable review question

Once you have selected your research topic or area, the next step is to narrow this down to a review question. This process is similar to a funnel or an inverted triangle (see Figure 2.1), where the wide base of the funnel represents the research topic and the narrow peak represents the specific research question. To illustrate this, a student nurse who is interested in the area of spinal deformities might select spinal deformities as the topic area, and one specific question arising from this specific topic could be 'the effectiveness of braces for treating patients with scoliosis'. Here the nurse has narrowed the topic area by specifying the particular treatment and also specifying the type of spinal deformity. Another nurse working in the accident and emergency (A&E) department may be very interested in the area of witnessed resuscitation (where family members are present during resuscitation attempts) as she has participated in a number of these procedures during her routine practice. 'Witnessed resuscitation' would then be the general topic area and a possible research (or review) question arising from this area could be 'What are the views of nurses regarding witnessed resuscitation in the A&E

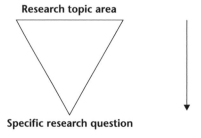

Research topic area

Specific research question

Figure 2.1   Deriving the research question from the topic area.

department?' Here the nurse has narrowed the topic area to a research question by specifying that she will be looking at nurses' views on this topic and will be restricting the study to the A&E department.

You may be asking how you actually derive the question from the topic. The way to do this is to ask a series of questions to narrow the topic down. To illustrate how this is done, we will use a hypothetical case study of a spinal nurse, Cheryl. Once you have read the case study you can try to narrow down your own topic area to a review question using the template provided in Box 2.2.

Case study: spinal nurse Cheryl

Cheryl is a spinal nurse working in a new spinal unit. As part of her role in the spinal deformity department, she takes care of many teenagers who suddenly develop a spinal deformity when they reach their teens, a condition known as adolescent idiopathic scoliosis (AIS). Before developing this deformity, when they were children, their spine was normal. The cause for this problem is not yet known so the treatment is concentrated on the symptoms. One of the treatments that Cheryl is involved in is bracing of the spinal curvatures to try to reduce these curvatures and rib hump. Many of these patients also have a number of psychological problems such as low self-esteem and self-image and occasionally pain. Cheryl would like to conduct a systematic review to find the evidence to underpin her practice.

Ten steps to help Cheryl develop the review question from her review topic
Cheryl starts developing her question by responding to the following ten steps.

1. Write down questions that have been in your mind from your area of practice. Choose questions about which you are very curious and to which you would love to know the answer.
   What are the effects of braces on the spinal curvature and rib hump?
   What are patients' experiences of wearing a brace?
   What are the positive effects of braces?
   What are the negative effects of braces?
   Are exercises for scoliosis effective?
   Is surgery for treating scoliosis effective?
   Is the practice of only observing and monitoring patients until they require surgery the best clinical practice?
2. Select one question that you would like to know the answer to.
   What are the effects of spinal braces on patients with adolescent idiopathic (no known cause) scoliosis?
3. Identify why it is interesting and worth investigating.
   If the brace is not effective at reducing the spinal curvature and rib hump, it may not be worth advising patients to use braces. It may also not be worth the sacrifices that adolescents have to make to wear them.
4. Identify issues related to the question.

Wearing a brace for 24 hours a day is not easy for teenagers. There are physical as well as psychological problems which need to be considered.

5 What will you gain by investigating the question?
When the patients come for treatment I can be assured that they are not making the sacrifice of wearing a brace for nothing, but that the brace is really effective in treating the spine and rib hump.

6 What will your profession or other professions and service users gain?
Both professionals and service users would be assured as to whether or not the treatment is an effective one. This would increase compliance and also has cost implications for health professionals.

7 What is the rationale for asking the question?
I would like to be sure the treatment we are providing to these children is actually working and that there is an evidence base for its effectiveness.

8 Why does it excite you?
It excites me because if the evidence is found to support the treatment effectiveness of bracing, then this may save a lot of young girls and boys the trauma of having spinal surgery in the future.

9 Is it a simple question or does it have several parts? If several parts, what are they?
This question has three parts. The treatment has both physical effects and psychological effects. The patients' and families' views are also very important.

10 In your opinion does the question address a significant problem? If so, answer the question 'So what?' here.
Yes, it would address a significant problem, as identified earlier on; there is a lack of evidence supporting the use of bracing. It would provide the evidence to support the judicious use of the brace in clinical practice.

Template to help you develop your review question from your review topic

Box 2.2 contains a template adapted from Bailey (1997) which you can use to help focus your own research question.

Once you have decided on a specific problem area and research question, the next step is to refine and break down the research question and make it as comprehensive and specific as possible. To do this you will need to consider the different categories of research questions: not only are there background and foreground questions, but also there are different types of foreground questions. Your review will differ based on whether you are investigating the effectiveness of a treatment programme, seeking to prevent a condition occurring, diagnosing a medical problem, looking at the cause or prognosis of a specific condition or disease, or exploring patients', users' or nurses' perceptions and experiences.

Box 2.2   Focusing the research question from the topic area

---

1   Write down three questions that have been in your mind from your area of practice. Choose questions about which you are very curious and to which you would love to know the answer.

2   Select one question that you would like to know the answer to.

3   Identify why it is interesting and worth investigating.

4   Identify issues related to the question.

5   What will you gain by investigating the question?

6   What will your profession or other professions and service users gain?

7   What is the rationale for asking the question?

8   Why does it excite you?

9   Is it a simple question or does it have several parts? If several parts, what are they?

10   In your opinion does the question address a significant problem? If so, answer the question 'So what?' here.

Using background or foreground questions: what is the difference?

Background questions refer to general nursing questions about a patient. These can be research questions about their medical condition such as: what causes the condition or how is it treated? The answers to these questions can be found in background sources such as textbooks or narrative reviews, which give an *overview* of the topic area.

Foreground questions answer a *specific* question about a specific topic. Foreground sources can be divided into primary sources such as original research articles published in peer-reviewed journals and secondary sources such as systematic reviews of the topic, and synopses and reviews of individual studies. Secondary sources are one step removed from the original research. Table 2.1 gives some examples of primary and secondary sources. The various concepts listed in the table will all be explained in this chapter.

Table 2.1   Types of studies in foreground sources

Primary sources – original research	Secondary sources – reviews of original research
• Experimental studies (an intervention is made)	• Systematic reviews
○ RCT	• Systematic reviews with a meta-analysis
○ Controlled trials	• Practice guidelines
• Observational studies (no intervention or variables are manipulated)	• Decision analysis
○ Cohort studies	• Consensus reports
○ Case-control studies	• Editorial, commentary
○ Case reports	
• Qualitative research studies	
○ Phenomenological, ethnographic or grounded theory studies	

Factors to consider when asking answerable and focused review questions

Blaikie (2007) suggests that the use of research or review questions is a neglected aspect in the design and conduct of research. He suggests that formulating a 'research question is the most critical and perhaps the most difficult part of any research design' (Blaikie 2007: 6). The formulation of the review question is crucial because the review question underpins all the aspects of the review methodology: every single step of the review is determined by the focused review question. The function of a review question can be summed up as follows:

- defines the nature and scope of the review
- identifies the keywords (together with the scoping search)

- determines the search strategy and the search to be undertaken
- provides guidance for selecting the primary research papers needed
- guides the data extraction and synthesis of the results.

When formulating a review question, it is important to ensure that you *ask an open question and not make a statement*. For example, rather than saying 'Braces improve the spinal curvatures of patients with scoliosis', as a novice student might, it would be preferable to ask, 'What effect do spinal braces have on patients with spinal curvatures?' In the first example you are making an assumption that braces will actually improve the back when they might not and they may even make the back worse. In this example you are making a statement and not asking a question. The first example is similar to a closed question and could introduce some bias (or errors). The second example is an open question and less biased. Asking this type of question will allow you to find research papers that discuss all the different effects of braces, both positive and negative.

Another issue to consider is the way you word a question: it is best *to avoid questions that can be answered with a simple yes or no*. For example, asking. 'Do braces have an effect on the spinal curvatures of patients with spinal deformities?' This can easily be answered with a yes or a no, whereas asking 'What effect do spinal braces have on patients with spinal curvatures?' encourages more discussion as well as being more open and unbiased. Table 2.2 lists some review questions to help you determine what sort of evidence you are looking for within the primary research papers that you will select to answer your review question. One way to facilitate the development of your review question is to determine what kind of question you are asking (Flemming 1998). From there you can work out what kind of evidence you are looking for.

Table 2.2 Main types of research questions

	Type	Description	Illustration
1	Treatment or therapy	Which treatment is most effective? Does it do more good than harm?	Is the use of dressing A better than dressing B in the treatment of venous leg ulcers?
2	Prevention	How to reduce the risk of disease	Do increasing levels of obesity increase the risk of developing diabetes?
3	Diagnosis	How to select and interpret diagnostic tests	Is having an X-ray as effective as having a computerized tomography (CT) scan for diagnosing a brain tumour?
4	Prognosis	How to anticipate the likely course of the disease	Are babies who are bottle fed more likely to be obese once they reach adulthood, compared to babies who are breastfed?
5	Causation	What are the risk factors for developing a certain condition?	Does exposure to parental alcohol during pregnancy increase the risk of foetal alcohol syndrome in newborn babies?
6	Patients' experiences and attitudes	How do people feel about this treatment or disease?	How do patients experience life with a venous leg ulcer?

Examples of the main types of research questions

Some examples from practice can be found below:

1 Examples of treatment or therapy questions
  - What are the effects of braces on patients with spinal deformities?
  - How effective are antidepressive medications on anxiety and depression?
2 Examples of prevention questions
  - For patients of 70 years and older, how effective is the use of the influenza vaccine at preventing flu as compared to patients who have not received the vaccine?
  - How effective is school screening for scoliosis at reducing the risk of future surgery in patients with scoliosis?
3 Examples of diagnosis questions
  - In patients with suspected anorexia nervosa, what is the accuracy of a new scale compared with the 'gold standard' previously validated instrument?
  - In patients with suspected scoliosis (spinal curvature), what is the accuracy of a new non-invasive surface tomography scanning device as compared to X-rays?
4 Examples of prognosis questions
  - How much more likely are babies who are bottle fed to catch colds than babies who are breastfed?
  - How much more likely are workers with musculoskeletal disorders to take sick leave as compared to workers diagnosed with stress?
  - How much more likely are children who are screened for scoliosis to have surgery than children who are not screened?
5 Examples of causation questions
  - For healthy post-menopausal patients on hormone replacement therapy (HRT), what are the increased risks for developing breast cancer?
  - In women taking oral contraceptives, is there an association between their use and breast cancer?
  - Does having a parent with a spinal deformity increase the risk of the child developing a scoliosis once they reach puberty?
6 Examples of patients' experiences and attitudes questions
  - What are teenagers' experiences of living with a spinal brace?
  - How do older patients experience life with cancer?
  - What are student nurses' experiences of life as a first-year university student?

Developing your review question further

If you have followed all of the steps above, you should by now have a tentative review question. In order to search for all the relevant papers on the topic, it is important that your question is both comprehensive and specific. It should include only one question and not two or three questions. A well-framed research question will have three or four elements (Flemming 1998). Once you have formulated your question the next step is to separate it into parts, as will be demonstrated in this section. The question formation usually includes identifying all the component parts, the population, the intervention, the comparative intervention (if any) and the outcomes that are measured. The acronym for this is PICO, which stands for population, intervention, comparative intervention and outcome. PICO is designed mainly for questions of therapeutic interventions (Khan et al. 2003). Another useful acronym is PEO, which stands for patient, exposure and outcome. PEO is used most frequently for qualitative questions (Khan et al. 2003).

A good way to identify the different parts of your question for PICO formats is to make a table containing four rows, one for each letter of the acronym. Table 2.3 shows what type of information to include in each of the sections. Table 2.4 shows some completed examples. For qualitative questions that use the PEO format you will need to create a table containing three rows. Table 2.5 shows you what to include in each of the sections.

In Tables 2.4 and 2.5 you can find some examples of using both the PICO and the PEO acronyms to formulate your own questions. The PICO questions are usually quantitative questions and the PEO ones are usually qualitative questions.

Regarding Cheryl's question from the case study, the structured question can be broken down into the component parts as defined by the PICO framework as follows:

- In patients with adolescent idiopathic scoliosis (P)
- how effective is bracing (I)
- as compared to observation (C)
- at reducing spinal curvature, rib hump and psychological problems (O)?

Table 2.6 shows how to separate the component parts of Cheryl's question using the PICO method.

Table 2.3 Component parts to consider when asking clear focused review questions

P Population and their problem	Here you need to state the clinical diagnosis or disease, the age, gender and any other relevant factors related to the population you would like to include. The population group needs to be specified whatever type of question you are considering.
I Intervention or exposure	If you are planning to evaluate a specific intervention you will need to state the type of intervention that you are seeking to evaluate, such as the type of drug and any specifics related to it like dosage and other relevant factors.
	If you are *not* looking at an intervention but are considering a specific 'exposure' (this term is used loosely) such as 'witnessed resuscitation' or 'domestic violence', you should use the E as in the PEO acronym instead of the PICO acronym.
C Comparative intervention	In a therapeutic question you will usually have a comparator (even if it is standard care). It is also possible to look at interventions without including a comparative intervention.
	For qualitative review questions or those involving a specific exposure or issue, this component is usually left out.
O Outcomes or themes	When writing down your outcomes, you need to consider the factors or issues you are looking for or measuring. For example, are you looking for any improvements in pain or mobility, or any other outcomes? With qualitative studies these will usually be the patients' experiences.

Table 2.4 Examples of using PICO to ask clear quantitative questions

	Example 1	*Example 2*	*Example 3*	*Example 4*
P Population and their problem	In patients with acute asthma	In children with a spinal deformity	In children with a fever	Among family members of patients with mental health problems
I Intervention or issue	how effective are antibiotics	how effective is bracing	how effective is paracetamol as compared to	how effective is listening to tranquil music, or audiotaped comedy routines
C Comparative intervention	as compared to standard care	as compared to observation	ibuprofen	as compared to standard care (none)
O Outcomes or themes	at reducing sputum production and coughing?	at reducing the scoliosis curvature?	at reducing fever and infection?	in reducing reported anxiety?

Table 2.5 Examples of using PEO to ask clear qualitative questions

	Example 1	*Example 2*	*Example 3*	*Example 4*
P Population and their problem	In teenagers with a spinal deformity	Older patients with cancer	Student nurses in their first year at university	Family members of patients with mental health problems
E Exposure	the development of a spinal deformity	cancer	studying to be a nurse at university and in their first year	having a family member with mental health problem
O Outcomes or themes	the patients' views	the patients' views	the students' views	the patients' views

Table 2.6 Cheryl's question broken down using the PICO method

P	I	C	O
Patients with adolescent idiopathic scoliosis	how effective is bracing	as compared to observation	at reducing spinal curvature, rib hump and psychological problems?

   Cheryl's nursing colleague Kirsty, who works in the same spinal unit, is more interested in the patients' views. Kirsty's question is 'What are the lived experiences of
patients with adolescent idiopathic scoliosis of having scoliosis and wearing a brace?'
Table 2.7 shows how Kirsty's question would be separated into its component parts
using the PEO method.

Table 2.7 Kirsty's question broken down using the PEO method

P	E	O
Patients with adolescent idiopathic scoliosis	having scoliosis and wearing a brace	lived experiences of having scoliosis and wearing a brace

---

Practice session 2.1

Now we have seen how to split different types of questions into their component parts, why don't you try to split your own question? Use the templates provided to divide your intervention or exposure question into PICO or PEO. If your question has more than one population group, please adapt the template as appropriate.

Box 2.3 Template for splitting a quantitative intervention question into PICO component parts

P	I	C	O

Box 2.4 Template for splitting a qualitative experience question into PEO component parts

P	E	O

Relating your question to the research design: what types of study designs should you look for to answer your research question?

Now that you have split your question into its component parts, the next step is to think about how your question relates to the research design of the studies that you plan to include within your review and which will form the basis for answering your review question. Why do we need this? Once you have formulated your question you will need to search for papers that answer your question. Khan et al. (2003) recommend the inclusion of the study designs of the proposed studies while still in the process of formulating your review question. So rather than using PICO or PEO you could adapt this to use PICOT or PEOT, where the T stands for the *type* of study or research design.

The type of research design can be thought of as the structure of the research study. It is a whole plan of how all the parts of the project fit together, including who the subjects are, what instruments were used if any, how the study was conducted and analysed and finally discussed.

Types of quantitative research designs

Some of the common quantitative research designs are described below.

Case reports and case series
A case report is a report of a treatment of an individual patient. Case reports are generally undertaken and reported when a patient of particular interest or with special or complex characteristics is treated by a nurse. For example, you may come across a patient who has a condition that you have never seen or heard of before and you are uncertain what to do. A search for case series or case reports may reveal information that will help you treat your patient. When the first case of Creutzfeldt-Jakob disease (CJD) was treated, it would have been reported as a case study. When a few cases are reported, this becomes a case series. Figure 2.2 illustrates the design of a case report study, with the schematic for a case report and case series research design.

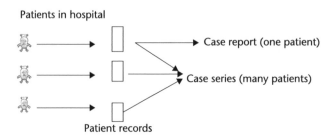

Figure 2.2 A schematic for a case report and case series.

Case control studies

Case control studies are research studies in which patients who already have a specific condition are compared with people who do not. They rely on medical records and patient recall for data collection. In other words they are retrospective studies (looking back) which can be done fairly quickly by taking the patients' histories. A good example of this can be seen by considering the time during the acquired immune deficiency syndrome (AIDS) epidemic when case control studies identified not only risk groups such as homosexual men, intravenous drug users and blood transfusion recipients but also risk factors, such as having multiple sex partners and not using condoms. Based on such studies, blood banks restricted high-risk individuals from donating blood, and educational programmes began to promote safer behaviours. As a result of these precautions, the speed of transmission of the human immunodeficiency virus (HIV) was greatly reduced, even before the virus had been identified (Schulz and Grimes 2002: 431). The schematic for a case control research design can be seen in Figure 2.3.

Cohort studies

Cohort studies are usually made up of a large population. The cohort study design follows patients who have a specific condition or who receive a particular treatment over time. These patients are compared with another group that has not been affected by the condition or treatment. For example, you may be interested in the long-term effects on nurses who smoke. In a cohort study you would follow up a group of nurses who smoke and a group who do not smoke and then compare their outcomes over time. One of the main problems with this design is that they can take a very long time to conduct. If you started following both groups of nurses when they were in their twenties and measured the outcomes every 10 years until they retired, this would mean the study would take over 40 years to complete. The schematic for a cohort research design can be seen in Figure 2.4.

Randomized controlled trials

Randomized controlled trials study the effect of treatments such as therapy, medication or programmes on real patients. The methods they include try to reduce the potential

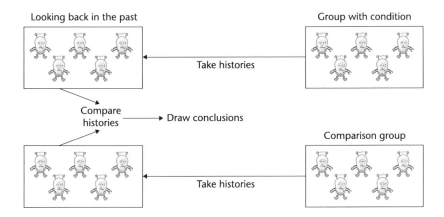

Figure 2.3 A schematic for a case control research design.

Group of interest – nurses who smoke

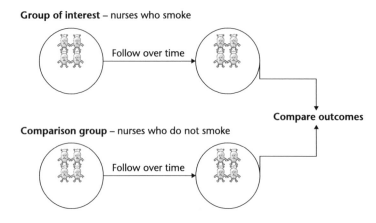

Comparison group – nurses who do not smoke

Figure 2.4 A schematic for a cohort research design.

for bias and the patients may be randomly assigned into a treated group and a control group. The inclusion of the control group, who have exactly the same conditions as the treated group with the exception of the treatment itself, allows us to ensure that it was the treatment itself that had an effect on the patients and not anything else. A schematic for an RCT research design can be seen in Figure 2.5.

Systematic reviews
As discussed in Chapter 1, an extensive literature search is conducted which uses only studies with sound methodology. The studies are collected, reviewed and assessed, data are extracted and the results summarized according to predetermined criteria of the review question (Figure 2.6).

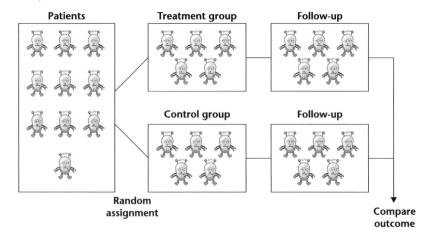

Figure 2.5 A schematic for an RCT research design.

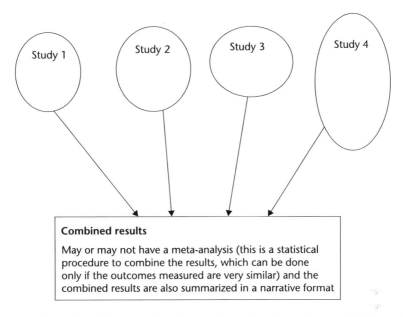

Figure 2.6   An illustration of how several studies can be combined to produce a definitive result.

Meta-analysis
A meta-analysis is a statistical procedure that is used in some systematic reviews. A meta-analysis examines a group of valid quantitative studies on a topic and combines the results using accepted statistical methodology to reach a consensus on the overall results. A meta-analysis can be used only on studies where the research papers included are very similar and where the outcome measures of the included research papers are the same. Only a small proportion of systematic reviews include a meta-analysis.

Types of qualitative research designs

The three most common types of qualitative research designs are described below.

Phenomenological research design
When nurses apply a phenomenological research design, they are concerned with the lived experiences of people (Greene 1997). This could be the lived experiences of patients with a particular condition, the experiences of older nurses, or the experiences of nursing students while training in hospitals.

Ethnographic research design
An ethnographic research design was originally used by anthropologists who went to live with native people in remote places in order to understand how they lived. According to Spradley (1979), ethnography is 'the work of describing a culture' and the goal of ethnographic research is 'to understand another way of life from the native point of view'

(Spradley 1979: 3). Within nursing practice, the term 'native' is used loosely and can refer to different nursing cultures that can be found within mental health nursing as compared to general and paediatric nursing. Spradley (1979: iv) suggests that ethnography is a useful tool for 'understanding how other people see their experience'. He emphasizes, however, that 'rather than *studying people*, ethnography means *learning from people*' (Spradley 1979: 3, my emphases). If we apply this in a nursing context, we may be interested in learning from nurses who work in a specific culture or area such as mental health nurses who work in prisons, nurses who work in an intensive care unit or nurses who work in palliative care.

Grounded theory research design

The grounded theory research design was developed by Glaser and Strauss (1967). This method is used as both a qualitative research method and a method of data analysis. In grounded theory the researcher aims to develop a theory that can explain events and behaviour, giving predictions and control over a situation. Grounded theory is a research method that operates almost in a reverse fashion from traditional research and at first may appear to be in contradiction to the scientific method. Rather than beginning with a hypothesis, the first step is data collection, through a variety of methods. From the data collected, the key points are marked with a series of themes or codes, which are extracted from the text. The codes or themes are grouped into similar *concepts* in order to make them more workable. From these concepts, *categories* are formed, which are the basis for the creation of a *theory*, or a reverse engineered hypothesis. This contradicts the traditional model of research, where the researcher chooses a theoretical framework, and only then applies this model to the phenomenon to be studied (Glaser and Strauss 1967).

Relating a specific research question to an appropriate research design

Having discussed the main types of quantitative and qualitative research designs, how does the specific type of research question relate to the appropriate research design? A summary of the types of research designs best suited to the different types of review questions can be found in Table 2.8.

Table 2.8 Summary of the types of research designs best suited to the different types of review questions

Type of question	Suggested best type of study			
	Least biased -_Most biased_			
Treatment or therapy	RCT >	cohort >	case control >	case series
Diagnosis	Retrospective, blind comparison to gold standard			
Aetiology or harm	RCT >	cohort >	case control >	case series
Prognosis		cohort >	case control >	case series
Prevention	RCT >	cohort >	case control >	case series
Experiences or perceptions	Qualitative studies: most common are phenomenological, ethnographic and grounded theory			

Questions of therapy, causes and prevention which can best be answered by RCT can also be answered by meta-analysis and systematic reviews.

Qualitative questions where a significant amount of research on the same research question has been conducted can also be answered by systematic reviews.

Key points

- Selecting a topic area for your systematic review is the first step towards undertaking the review.
- The specific topic you select may arise from a number of different triggers.
- Once you have selected your research topic, the next step is to narrow this down to a specific research question.
- There are two main types of questions: background questions which are general nursing questions and foreground questions which answer a specific question about a specific topic.
- Foreground questions and sources can be divided into primary sources such as original research and secondary sources such as systematic reviews.
- Formulating research questions is the most critical and perhaps the most difficult part of any research design.
- The research question underpins all the components of the review methods.
- It is important to ensure that you ask an open question.
- It is best to avoid closed questions that can be answered with a simple yes or no.
- The main types of research questions relate to treatment or therapy, prevention, diagnosis, prognosis, causation and experiences.
- It is important that your question is both comprehensive and specific.
- A well-framed research question will have three or four elements.
- The question formation usually includes identifying all the component parts: the population, the intervention or exposure, the comparative intervention (if any) and the outcomes that are measured. The acronym for these are PICO or PEO.
- It is important to match your question to the appropriate research design.
- The research design can be thought of as the structure of the research study.

Summary

This chapter discussed the different ways of finding topic areas for your review and described the meaning and functions of an answerable and focused review question. The chapter presented the main types of focused research questions together with some examples from nursing practice provided. The chapter discussed the different types of research questions and the importance of selecting the appropriate research design for the type of research question you have selected. A number of templates were provided to help you formulate your own answerable and focused systematic review question.

3 Writing the plan and background to your review

Overview

- The importance of writing a plan for your review
- Steps to take when planning your review
- Sections to include within your plan
- Background to your plan
- Providing an operational definition of the clinical problem
- Highlighting the importance of the review question and grabbing the attention of the reader
- Clarifying the gap in systematic reviews in the clinical area
- Using different tools and methods to help you start writing up your background section
- The importance of managing and planning your time

The importance of writing a plan for your review

Writing a plan of what you intend to include before you start your systematic review is very important. A plan (also called a 'protocol') describes in advance the review question and your rationale for the proposed methods you will use. It also includes details of how different types of studies will be located, appraised and synthesized (Petticrew and Roberts 2006). Describing your methods in advance is a way of trying to minimize bias (something that causes a consistent deviation from the truth) as you cannot start changing the way you review the papers once you see the results of the identified studies. For instance, if you said in the plan that you will be including only randomized controlled trials (RCTs) and then found a study by a well-known nurse or healthcare professional which was not an RCT, the temptation might be for you to include it. However, you would not be able to do this as you have stated otherwise in your protocol. Another important reason to undertake a plan for your review is that you can then show this to other colleagues you work with, patients with the specific problem and/or your supervisor. They can read your plan and provide you with further suggestions to improve it, as you may not have thought of relevant issues that are important to the patients, service users and other nurses and healthcare professionals.

While most nurses who are conducting their first review will conduct it on their own, the highest quality systematic reviews, such as those undertaken by the Cochrane Centre and the Campbell Collaboration, are usually undertaken in teams. Conducting a review in a team decreases bias and increases the validity (or truthfulness) of the results. If you are a student nurse or a clinician without access to a team, it is perfectly acceptable to conduct a review on your own, so long as you acknowledge that doing so may decrease the validity of your results and increase the level of bias in your study.

Steps to take when planning your review

Once you have formulated your review question, it is a good idea to undertake a quick general search (also called a scoping search) to make sure that there are no systematic literature reviews already available or in progress that have already addressed your review question. Box 3.1 shows some common websites where you can check this out (please note that this list is not exhaustive). An excellent checklist is in a book called *Systematic Reviews* available for free on the Centre for Reviews and Dissemination website (see below).

Box 3.1   Websites for checking for systematic literature reviews

- Cochrane Centre and Library
  http://cochrane.co.uk/en/clib.html
- TRIP Database
  www.tripdatabase.com
- Centre for Reviews and Dissemination (University of York)
  www.york.ac.uk/inst/crd
- Campbell Collaboration
  www.campbellcollaboration.org
- Cochrane Qualitative Research Methods Group
  www.cqrmg.cochrane.org

If you find a narrative review that was published recently, it is fine to go ahead with your systematic literature review, because a systematic review is considered to be a much higher quality review. If you find a systematic literature review exactly like the one you plan to carry out, there are a number of strategies you can follow; for example, you can look to see if the review you found in your preliminary search was conducted recently or a number of years previously. If a number of papers have been published since the last systematic review, it is still fine to go ahead with your own systematic review as your review will contribute new knowledge. If no new papers have been published since the last systematic review, there is no point in conducting a review that would produce exactly the same results. The best thing to do in this case is to change or 'tweak' the population group, the intervention or the outcomes, so your specific review question will be slightly different from the previously published systematic review. For example, in Cheryl's case, her title is 'The effect of braces as compared to other interventions (exercise or surgery) on adolescents with idiopathic scoliosis'. If she found a systematic literature review that had already been conducted and no new papers had been published since, she could change the population group and look at adults. Alternatively she could look at a subgroup of the population, such as obese adolescents, or change the intervention, comparative group or specific outcomes to be investigated.

Practice session 3.1

For your own review question, search the websites to identify if your research question has already been addressed through a systematic review.

- Cochrane Centre and Library
  http://cochrane.co.uk/en/clib.html
- TRIP Database
  www.tripdatabase.com
- Centre for Reviews and Dissemination
  www.york.ac.uk/inst/crd
- Campbell Collaboration
  www.campbellcollaboration.org
- Cochrane Qualitative Research Methods Group
  www.cqrmg.cochrane.org

Sections to include within your plan

The length and time you devote to writing up your plan depends on the specific circumstances in which you are writing your review. If you are writing up the review to answer a research question for yourself, it is acceptable for the plan of your review to be quite brief and sketchy. If you are planning a more formal review, for instance if you are conducting this review as part of your continuing professional development, or if it is a requirement for a module on a formal nursing programme, such as a dissertation, the plan of your review will need to be more detailed and precise.

The sections within the plan and in the full review are identical, except that in the plan, the sections are quite brief and will not include the results and discussion sections of the review. Once you have written your plan and are completing the full review, you will need to go over each section in more detail and include your results and discussion sections as well.

A brief overview of all the sections to include within your plan (and later your full review) is listed below. Chapters 4–7 provide a much more detailed discussion of the full process to conduct each section of the review. Full details for undertaking each part of the review can be found in the chapter indicated.

- Developing an answerable review question (Chapter 2)
- Writing the background to your review (briefly) (Chapter 3)
- Writing the objectives (or purpose of the review) (Chapter 4)
- Specifying your inclusion and exclusion criteria (Chapter 5)
- Conducting the search strategy (Chapter 5)
- Selecting, appraising and extracting the relevant data from your research papers to answer your review question (Chapter 6).

Developing a review question has already been discussed in Chapter 2. The background section is discussed in this chapter and the remaining points will be discussed in Chapters 4–7. A brief summary of what should be included in each section of your review plan is found below.

Writing the background to your review (briefly)

The background section of a systematic review is similar to writing a narrative review. The purpose of the background section is to provide an overview of the specific area of the review, highlight the clinical problems associated with the area or question, discuss the relevant reviews within the specific clinical area and clarify the gap in systematic reviews in this area.

Writing the objectives (or purpose of the review)

The purpose of writing out the objectives of your review is to clarify your reason for conducting the review. If we go back to the review on braces, we defined our objective as follows: 'The purpose of our review was to evaluate the effectiveness of braces on patients with spinal curvature and rib hump'.

Specifying your inclusion and exclusion criteria

In this section you need to decide on the specific criteria by which you plan to select (or not select) the primary papers for your review. These will include specific criteria on the types of subjects, interventions (or exposure), comparative group and outcomes, and the types of studies you plan to include.

Conducting the search strategy

The search strategy describes how and where you plan to search for your primary research papers to include for your review. To ensure that your search strategy is replicable, it is important to include a detailed description of your search strategy which is based on your review question.

Selecting, appraising and extracting the relevant data from your research papers to answer your review question

In this section you describe the process of how you plan to select your papers, how you plan to evaluate your papers, what framework you will be using to do this, and finally the process of extracting data from your papers to answer the review question. In other words you will be explaining in detail how you are planning to go through your papers and take out the relevant information to answer your review question. For example, if you were interested in looking at the effectiveness of the Weight Watchers diet or eating programme, you would want to know the weight of the participants in all your papers before they started on Weight Watchers, as well as after finishing the programme. You would read through all your research papers to find the figures that address this and 'extract' them. Full details of how to do this are described in Chapter 5.

Background to your protocol

The role of the background in your protocol (and later in the review) is to describe the setting and context of the area of research, the importance of the topic and the reasons why it has been chosen (Cochrane Collaboration 2002). There may be a number of reasons for the choice of topic, for example reporting a review to evaluate the effectiveness of a particular treatment or replicating an important review in a particular area of practice carried out in another country or a number of years previously.

A well-written background should be clear about the direction of the study. In the background, it is important to explain what reviews have already been conducted in this area, if any, discuss their strengths and limitations, and describe how the proposed review will fill a gap in the literature, providing new information that could advance practice (Cochrane Collaboration 2009).

It is important not to be too anecdotal in recounting the reasons for conducting the review. Back up your reasons with facts and figures and references where possible. For an intervention study, the background could include some or all of the following, depending on the specific topic of your review:

1   Provide an operational definition of the clinical problem.
2   Cite research papers or government documents with statistical figures to highlight the importance of the study.
3   Describe the signs and symptoms (or consequences) of the disease, illness, problem or issue.
4   Provide details of the patients' age, gender and other pertinent details.
5   Describe the course of the disease or pathophysiology.
6   If the review is related to the effectiveness of any type of intervention, there needs to be a discussion about how the disease or issue is usually managed in practice.
7   Describe the general outcome measures.

8   Once the problem has been discussed, including incidence, effect on patients' lives and management, a gap of systematic reviews in the evidence or literature needs to be identified. References should be used to support how the proposed review is different.

Remember that you are trying to show that there is a gap in systematic literature reviews and not in primary research papers or narrative reviews. Some of the key issues will now be discussed individually and in more depth.

Providing an operational definition of the clinical problem

When starting the background section it is usual to provide an 'operational definition' of the clinical problem you are addressing in your review. An operational definition is a clear, concise, detailed definition of a measure described within a particular context; here you will be stating what the problem is and what it is not. Once you have provided an operational definition and if your issue relates to a clinical problem, it is usually appropriate to describe the following: the causes of the condition, the age of your specific population group, the specific diagnosis, the signs and symptoms of the illness or problem, and the natural history or course of the disease or pathophysiology.

In Cheryl's example on 'Bracing for adolescents with scoliosis', in her background section, Cheryl needs to provide an operational definition of the term 'adolescent idiopathic scoliosis (AIS)' to clarify the nature of the clinical problem. Cheryl could write something like the paragraph below. After every statement, it is important to include a reference to demonstrate that this piece of information has been obtained from a reliable source.

> Adolescent Idiopathic Scoliosis is a deformity of the spine and rib cage which generally occurs in children and adolescents between the ages of 10–16 years old (Parent 2005). The causes of AIS are not known though many theories have been put forward over the years; these include possible genetic, muscular or neurological causes among others (Scoliosis Research Society (SRS) 2007).

Highlighting the importance of the review question and grabbing the attention of the reader

There are a number of ways to clarify the importance of the research or clinical problem, including the use of statistics, key government papers and previous important research work in the area. The use of statistics highlights the importance of the problem within the general population. The statement 'Low back pain occurs in 80 per cent of the population at some time in their lives' makes it clear that low back pain is an important clinical problem. Citing key government documents within your background is a good strategy as it demonstrates the importance that government bodies allocate to this specific area of health. For example, Cheryl could write something like this:

The incidence of AIS varies between different countries from 0.9 to 12 per cent (Parent 2005). AIS occurs much more frequently in girls and for curves of over 30 degrees and the occurrence of adolescent idiopathic scoliosis in girls as compared to boys is approximately 8:2 or four times greater (Bates 2010).

In the example above, the statement that AIS can occur in up to 12 per cent of children and mainly in girls is highlighting that this is an important problem that needs to be reviewed. Once the importance of the topic has been clarified, the signs and symptoms of the clinical condition could be discussed. In Cheryl's example, she could say something like this:

The deformity results in a spinal curvature together with a rib hump and shoulder, waist and pelvic asymmetries (Lonstein 2006). This deformity has a significant impact on these young children and adolescents. These include a decreased quality of life as well as many psychological problems such as low self-esteem and self-image (Maclean 1989; Freidel 2002).

Once Cheryl has discussed the clinical problem together with the resultant signs and symptoms of the condition, it is appropriate for her to discuss the current management for patients with AIS.

Patients with AIS are generally treated to prevent the curvature and rib hump getting any worse. The treatment type depends on the severity of the curvature and rib hump. For small curves (10–30 degrees) either annual monitoring and observation or scoliosis-specific exercises are usually recommended. Curves between 30 and 50 degrees are usually braced or observed and curves over 50 degrees are usually recommended for surgery.

Clarifying the gap in systematic reviews in the clinical area

Describing and briefly critiquing previous reviews that have been conducted in your specific review area is important. You need to show that your systematic review has not been conducted before and that yours is the most up-to-date and best quality review. If narrative reviews have been conducted in your specific area, it is worth mentioning them but explaining that as they are narrative reviews the results may be biased. If there are previous systematic reviews you would like to include, you should provide a brief description and explain what was reviewed and when, and then very clearly point out how your review is different from these. In other words you are attempting to clarify the gap in systematic reviews in the literature.

This is important because your aim is to prove that your systematic review is actually needed. If an identical review was carried out over a year ago and no primary papers in this area have been published since then, it is clear that a systematic review would not be needed. In order to show the gap in systematic reviews in your specific area, you now need to describe what other reviews have been conducted, whether they were narrative or systematic reviews, how long ago they were conducted, and to what extent your review is similar or different. Returning to Cheryl's example:

> To date, reviews in this area have been mostly narrative reviews which have not included the evaluation of the methodological quality of the included studies and have not included all relevant primary papers. For example, the narrative review by Chan (2003) did not include all primary papers in the area and the narrative review by Ottenburger (2007) did not evaluate the methodological quality of the included primary papers. One systematic review was found but this related to the effect of braces on adults and not adolescents with idiopathic scoliosis. A 'gold standard' systematic review is needed to make sure that the 'sacrifices that children are making when wearing a brace are indeed worthwhile' (Negrini 2010: 3).

All the above excerpts are based on a Cochrane Review on *Braces for Idiopathic Scoliosis in Adolescents*, which I undertook together with a team of international researchers (Negrini et al. 2010). Should you wish to read the whole background of this review you can find it at: http://onlinelibrary.wiley.com/doi/10.1002/14651858.CD006850.pub2/pdf. Cheryl's examples are based on this review, but I would like to clarify that I have added or changed some sentences in order to illustrate a point or make an argument. In our case no systematic reviews that specifically addressed the effectiveness of braces on adolescents with idiopathic scoliosis had as yet been undertaken.

Using different tools and methods to help you start writing up your background section

There are a number of different tools that you can use to help you write up the background section of your review. In the case study, Cheryl is aware that if she begins writing too soon she will be forced to stop and go back to the initial steps. Cheryl has searched widely and has read a number of review papers, government documents and research papers in the general area of AIS. She has also been trying to identify what is known and what is not known about her topic. She will begin to write her protocol only when she is confident that she can answer 'Yes' to the six questions listed in Practice session 3.2.

Practice session 3.2		
Have you searched and read broadly in the area of your specific review question?	YES ☐	NO ☐
Have you made sure that a number of primary research papers have been conducted relating to your specific area of interest?	YES ☐	NO ☐
Have you spent time thinking critically about your specific review topic?	YES ☐	NO ☐
Have you spent time discussing your review topic with your colleagues or supervisor with a knowledge of this area?	YES ☐	NO ☐
Have you found out how people in other disciplines think about your research topic?	YES ☐	NO ☐
Do you feel ready to begin writing your research protocol?	YES ☐	NO ☐

Before you start writing the background to your review, it is important that you have read around the area and spoken to your colleagues or supervisors about it. Creating a mind map, making lists and brainstorming are useful tools to get you started. Try answering the questions to Practice session 3.2 before you start to check that you are ready to start writing your background.

Many clinicians and students undertaking a systematic literature review in nursing for the first time are unsure about how and where to start. A good way round this is to try to draw a mind map. Mind mapping is a process of representing 'concepts' or knowledge structures used in learning in a two-dimensional graphic arrangement and includes the labelling and linking of concepts to form associations or hierarchies. The centre represents the hub or central theme.

By presenting ideas in a radial, graphical, non-linear manner, mind maps encourage a brainstorming approach to planning and organizational tasks (Rooda 1994). Brainstorming is a creativity technique in which a group of people try to find a solution for a specific problem by gathering a list of ideas spontaneously contributed by its members.

Although Cheryl could do this activity on her own, she decides to get together with a group of her colleagues (as they may have ideas and thoughts about the topic that she may not have thought about) to begin drawing a mind map on the topic of braces for scoliosis (Figure 3.1).

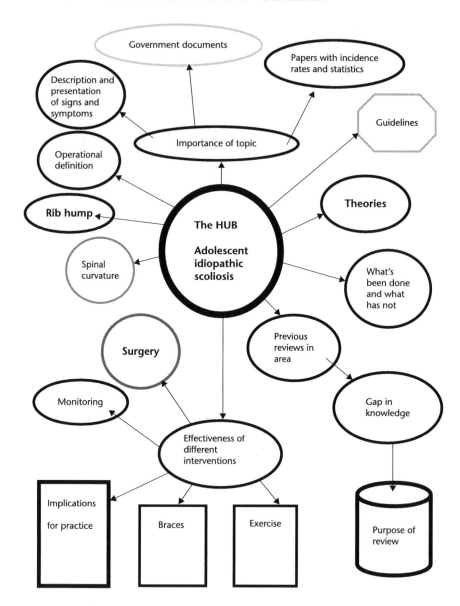

Figure 3.1   Example of a mind map that Cheryl could make on her topic of braces for scoliosis.

Practice session 3.3

Try to make a mind map for your own review topic here.

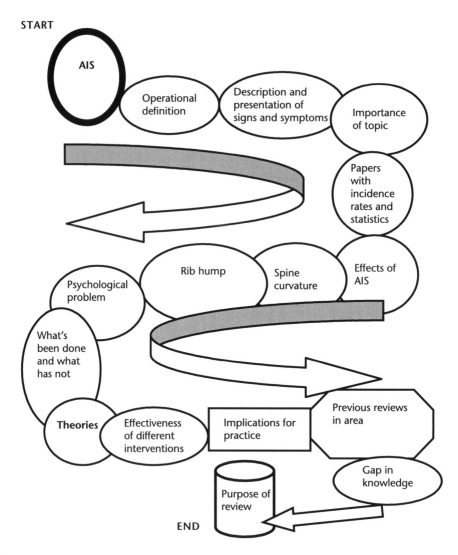

START

AIS

Operational definition

Description and presentation of signs and symptoms

Importance of topic

Papers with incidence rates and statistics

Rib hump

Spine curvature

Effects of AIS

Psychological problem

What's been done and what has not

Theories

Effectiveness of different interventions

Implications for practice

Previous reviews in area

Gap in knowledge

Purpose of review

END

Figure 3.2 Cheryl organizes her mind map in the order she plans to write it up.

Practice session 3.4

Try to organize your mind map in the order that you plan to write it out.

Alternative template

If you prefer, you can use a list instead of a mind map to write the topics you would like to include in your background, listing each issue one beneath the other in the same order that you will write them in your own background.

An example is listed below:

1   Definition of AIS
2   Description and presentation
3   Importance of topic
4   Effect on people's lives
5   Previous research in area
6   Theories
7   Effectiveness of different interventions
8   Gap in knowledge
9   Purpose.

Box 3.2 is a template for you to list all the points for your own background.

Box 3.2   Template for listing the points for your own background

1

2

3

4

5

6

7

8

9

Once Cheryl has made a list of all the concepts, she decides to add another column to her list. In this column she writes all the possible sources of information that she may require and makes sure that they are available nearby so she can refer to them as she writes. Table 3.1 on page 46 shows Cheryl's new list. Box 3.3 provides a template for you to list your own themes and possible sources of information.

Box 3.3 Template for listing your own themes and possible sources of information

	Themes	Possible sources of information
1	Operational definition	
2		
3		
4		
5		
6		
7		
8		
9		

Table 3.1 Cheryl's themes and possible sources of information

	Themes	Possible sources of information and activities to do
1	Definition of AIS	Dictionary
		Government documents
		Review documents
		Research papers
2	Description and presentation	As above
3	Importance of topic	Papers with statistics and incidence rates
		Government health department documents
4	Effect on people's lives	All above, especially research papers and reviews
5	Previous research in area	Research papers and systematic reviews or other reviews that have done research in a similar or related area
6	Theories	Theoretical papers or research papers primarily
7	Effectiveness of different interventions	Research papers showing effectiveness of different intervention studies
8	Gap in knowledge	All above, highlighting what has and has not been done yet
9	Purpose	This will address the gap above

The importance of managing and planning your time

Conducting a systematic review is a time-consuming process and it is vital that you set aside enough time to conduct it. If you are writing a systematic review dissertation, you will have been given specific criteria to write this and you will need a significant period (2–3 months minimum) depending on how much time you can devote to conducting it and writing it up. If you are conducting a systematic review as part of your continuing professional development, you should set aside at least 3–4 months just to write your plan and protocol and then possibly another 6–12 months to conduct it and write it all up. I usually advise my students to make a timetable of all the activities involved and set a deadline for each activity. A Gantt chart is a useful tool to use and can help significantly in making sure you stick to your deadlines (see Table 3.2). You can use the Gantt chart in Box 3.4 for your own systematic review; you may want to change the word 'weeks' to 'months'.

Key points

- Writing a plan of what you intend to include before you start your systematic review is very important.
- A plan describes in advance the review question and your rationale for the proposed methods you will use. It also includes details of how different types of studies will be located, appraised and synthesized.

Table 3.2 Example of a Gantt chart

Weeks	1	2	3	4	5	6	7	8	9
Select an area and carry out background reading	▨	▨							
Develop a question		▨	▨						
Write the background			▨	▨	▨				
Write the objectives					▨				
Write the criteria					▨				
Select your studies						▨			
Appraise your studies						▨	▨		
Extract data						▨	▨		
Write results							▨	▨	
Write discussion								▨	▨
Write up paper or dissertation								▨	▨

- Once you have formulated your review question, it is a good idea to undertake a quick general search (also called a scoping search) to make sure that there are no systematic literature reviews already available or in progress that have addressed your review question.
- A plan includes all of the following sections:
  - An answerable review question.
  - The background to the review.
  - The objectives of the review.
  - The inclusion and exclusion criteria.
  - The search strategy.
  - The proposed methods for selecting, appraising and extracting the relevant data from your research papers to answer your review question.
- The background in the protocol (and later in the review) is to describe the setting and context of the area of research, the importance of the topic and the reasons why it has been chosen. In the background section of your protocol, you may consider including some of the following:
  - Provide an operational definition of the clinical problem.
  - Cite research papers or government documents with statistical figures to highlight the importance of the study.
  - Describe the signs and symptoms of the disease.
  - Provide details of the patients' age, gender and other pertinent details.
  - Describe the course of the disease.
  - If the review is related to the effectiveness of any type of intervention, there needs to be a discussion about how the disease or issue is usually managed in practice.
  - Describe the general outcome measures.

Box 3.4 Template Gantt chart for your own systematic review

Weeks	1	2	3	4	5	6	7	8	9
Select an area and carry out background reading									
Develop a question									
Write the background									
Write the objectives									
Write the criteria									
Select your studies									
Appraise your studies									
Extract data									
Write results									
Write discussion									
Write up paper or dissertation									

- ○ A systematic review gap in the evidence or literature needs to be identified.
- ○ References should be used to support how the proposed review is different.
- There are a number of different tools such as mind maps and lists that you can use to help you write up the background section of your review.

Summary

This chapter discussed the key factors that need to be considered when writing a plan for your systematic literature review. The different sections within the plan were briefly described and examples provided. The first stage of the plan, the background, was discussed in more detail and excerpts included to clarify this process. Different tools and methods were suggested to help you start writing up the background section of your plan.

4 Specifying your objectives and inclusion and exclusion criteria

Overview

- Clarifying the preliminaries: problem statement, review question, aims and objectives
- Stating your aims and objectives
- Issues to consider when writing your problem statement, aims, objectives, review question and title
- Specifying the inclusion and exclusion criteria for selecting your primary research papers

Clarifying the preliminaries: problem statement, review question, aims and objectives

To avoid making mistakes when undertaking a review, it is important to be clear regarding the precise meaning and the differences between a problem statement, a review question, an aim and an objective. Depending on which papers or books you read, these terms may sometimes be used interchangeably. This occurs quite frequently with the terms 'objectives' and 'aims', which actually have slightly different meanings.

A problem statement is usually a simple statement of 'what is'. For example, 'It is not known if treatment 1 or treatment 2 is more effective for treating adult patients with chronic obstructive pulmonary disease (COPD)'. A problem statement means that you are simply *stating* a problem.

The review question usually follows from the problem. This involves changing the problem statement into a review question. Consider this problem statement: 'It is not known if treatment 1 or treatment 2 is more effective for treating adult patients with COPD'. To change this statement into a review question, all you need to do is rephrase the statement into a question like this: 'Is treatment 1 or treatment 2 more effective in treating adult patients with COPD?' The easiest way to do this is to use similar or even identical terminology to ensure that there is no change in meaning between the problem statement and the review question.

Once you have written the review question, how are the aims and objectives derived? In most dictionaries you will find that the terms 'aim' and 'objective' are synonyms (i.e. words meaning the same thing), with both terms referring to the purpose for doing something. Within the area of research methodology, these terms tend to be used for different types of research. The term 'aim' is usually used to state the purpose of a study within qualitative research studies while the term 'objective' is generally used in quantitative research. You will find when you have read numerous papers that this is not always the case and in many reviews these terms are also used interchangeably.

The 'aim' of a project is to solve the problem and answer the question, and is usually a general statement (Jenkins et al. 1998), while the term 'objective' is more specific than the aim. The objectives usually state what the researcher is going to do. For every aim, there are usually two or more objectives. In the example above, 'Is treatment 1 or treatment 2 more effective in treating adult patients with COPD?', there are a number of activities that the researcher will need to do. Referring to Cheryl's example, an aim is a more general statement while the objectives are much more specific (see Box 4.1).

Box 4.1   Cheryl's example relating to the effectiveness of treatments for adolescent patients with scoliosis

Problem statement
It is not known if treatment 1 or treatment 2 is more effective for treating adolescent patients with scoliosis.

Review question
Is treatment 1 or treatment 2 more effective for treating adolescent patients with scoliosis?

Aim
The aim of this study is to evaluate if there is a difference between treatment 1 and treatment 2 for adolescent patients with scoliosis.

Objectives

- Collect data on the effectiveness of treatment 1 and treatment 2
- Compare the effectiveness of the two treatments
- Compare the findings of this study with other studies
- Provide guidelines for helping adolescent patients with scoliosis.

Title of review
A systematic literature review comparing the effectiveness of treatment 1 to treatment 2 for treating adolescent patients with scoliosis.

Stating your aims and objectives

Once you have written a first draft of the background for your review, you will need to state the aim or aims and the objectives for your own review. It is important that the aims and objectives include all the PICO (or PEO) elements in the same way as they are included for the review question.

Let's refer back to Cheryl's question: 'In patients with adolescent idiopathic scoliosis how effective is bracing as compared to other treatments at reducing spinal curvature, rib hump and psychological problems?' Cheryl's aim is to solve this problem and answer the question. Cheryl's aim becomes 'The aim of this review is to evaluate the effectiveness of bracing as compared to all other treatments at reducing spinal curvature, rib hump and psychological problems'. The main difference between the review question and the aim is that the former is a question and the latter is a statement.

Before Cheryl writes her objectives, she has to consider what she will need to do in order to conduct the review. Cheryl's objectives could be, for example:

- Search for papers on the effectiveness of braces and all other treatments
- Collect data on the effectiveness of braces and all other treatments
- Compare primary papers on the effectiveness of the treatments above
- Compare the findings of this review with other reviews
- Provide guidelines on the effectiveness of the different treatments for helping adolescent patients with scoliosis.

Case study: intensive care nurse Sue

Sue is an experienced qualified nurse working in an intensive care unit. She has seen a number of patients who have been brought in following severe accidents and have been resuscitated. She has witnessed the grief that relatives experienced, which was exacerbated when they had not been allowed to be with their loved ones during this traumatic event. This was made worse if their relative died and they had not been present during the attempted resuscitation. Sue decided to conduct a systematic review on this subject as part of her professional development.

Case study: A&E nurse Mary

Mary is a newly qualified nurse working in accident and emergency, who often sees women who have been physically abused and brought in with severe facial and body bruises. This has led her to become interested in the area of domestic violence. Her review question is: 'For women who have experienced domestic violence, how effective are advocacy programmes as compared to routine treatments on women's quality of life (as measured by a specific validated scale)?'

Mary's aim will be similar to her question, for example: 'The aim of this review is to evaluate the effectiveness of advocacy programmes as compared to other treatments on the quality of life of women victims of domestic violence'. As you can see in both the question and the aim, Mary has stated the population, the intervention, the comparative intervention and the outcomes. The next step is for her to write out her objectives. Like Cheryl, Sue and Mary need to consider all the activities they will be doing in order to conduct their systematic literature reviews so Mary's objectives could be:

- Search for papers on the effectiveness of advocacy programmes and other treatments
- Collect data on the effectiveness of advocacy programmes and other treatments
- Compare primary papers on the different treatments
- Compare the findings of this review with other reviews
- Provide guidelines for helping women victims of domestic violence.

Issues to consider when writing your problem statement, aims, objectives, review question and title

It is important when writing your review to ensure that you are always saying the same thing when writing out the title, the problem statement, the review question, the aim and objectives. A common mistake among student nurses I have taught is that they have used different terms when writing out each of the above, resulting in the title and aims being different. You will notice in the two examples in Tables 4.1 and 4.2 that the same words are used throughout.

Once you have done this, use the template in Practice session 4.1 to write the problem statement, review question, aim, objectives and title for your own review.

Table 4.1 Mary's example on domestic violence (quantitative review)

Problem statement	Little is known on the effectiveness of advocacy programmes as compared to other treatments on women's quality of life for women who have experienced domestic violence.
Review question	For women who have experienced domestic violence, how effective are advocacy programmes as compared to other treatments on women's quality of life?
Aim	The aim of this study is to evaluate the effectiveness of advocacy programmes as compared to other treatments on women's quality of life for women who have experienced domestic violence.
Objectives	• Search for papers on the effectiveness of advocacy programmes and other treatments • Collect data on the effectiveness of advocacy programmes and other treatment • Compare the primary papers on the different treatments • Compare the findings of this review with other reviews • Provide guidelines for helping women who have experienced domestic violence.
Title	A systematic literature review on the effectiveness of advocacy programmes, as compared to other treatments on women's quality of life, for women who have experienced domestic violence

Table 4.2 Sue's example on witnessed resuscitation (qualitative review)

Problem statement	Little is known on the lived experience of patients, family members and healthcare professionals on family presence during resuscitation and/or invasive procedures.
Review question	Family presence during resuscitation and/or invasive procedures: what is the lived experience of patients, family members and healthcare professionals?
Aim	The aim of this systematic review is to evaluate the lived experience of patients, family members and healthcare professionals regarding family presence during resuscitation and/or invasive procedures.
Objectives	• Search for papers on the lived experience of patients, family members and healthcare professionals • Collect data on the lived experience of patients, family members and healthcare professionals • Compare the lived experiences of the different healthcare professionals • Compare the findings of this review with other reviews • Provide guidelines for helping women who have experienced domestic violence.
Title	A systematic literature review on family presence during resuscitation and/or invasive procedures: the lived experience of patients, family members and healthcare professionals.

Practice session 4.1

Write down the problem statement, review question, aim, objectives and title for your own review question.

Problem statement

Review question

Aim

Objectives

Title

When you have filled in all the details for your own review question, read them through again to make sure that for each section you are stating the same thing. It may be worth giving it to a colleague to read to see if he or she agrees with you.

Specifying the inclusion and exclusion criteria for selecting your primary research papers

Stating your inclusion and exclusion criteria before you conduct the review is important. This section is where you describe the criteria that you will be using to include any research studies in your review. Torgerson (2003) suggests that a high quality systematic review should have inclusion and exclusion criteria that are 'rigorously and transparently reported *a priori* (before you start the review)' (Torgerson 2003: 26). You may well ask 'Why is this necessary?' The reason is so that your search can target the papers that will answer your question and exclude any irrelevant ones. The criteria need to be explicit and applied stringently (Torgerson 2003). The criteria you select should follow from the research question, keeping in mind the PICO or PEO format. You will need to describe the types of research studies (T) you will be including, the participants, interventions, comparative groups (if any) and outcome measures. PICO now becomes PICOT. For qualitative systematic reviews use PEO (which will now become PEOT). Please note that whether you are writing a qualitative or quantitative review, all of these steps are the same with the exception that for qualitative reviews the data extraction and presentation of results are conducted a little differently from quantitative reviews. Further details on these differences can be found in Chapters 7 and 8. How to specify the inclusion and exclusion criteria for each component (PICOT or PEOT) of your review question will now be discussed.

Specifying the types of studies to be included and excluded

When selecting your primary research papers, it is important to select papers with the appropriate design for your particular review question. If you are evaluating the effectiveness of an intervention, the highest quality research designs will be randomized controlled trials or clinical controlled trials (CCTs). (Please refer to the research design section in Chapter 2 to go over the different research designs if you are still uncertain about this.) You could also use other research designs that do not include a control intervention, but these will be lower on the hierarchical scale of quality of evidence (see Chapter 2).

In the Cochrane systematic review that I conducted with an international team of colleagues, we included both RCTs and CCTs; we also included prospective cohort studies because we knew there were not many RCTs (Negrini et al. 2010).

In the case studies, Cheryl and Mary will be seeking similar papers as they are looking at conducting quantitative reviews on the effectiveness of interventions. They have excluded case studies, because case studies are very low down on the quality of evidence scale. If there was very little information available, however, it may be worth considering the inclusion of case studies designs.

In contrast, Sue will be evaluating people's lived experiences of witnessed resuscitation and will be conducting a qualitative review. If you plan to conduct a qualitative review, you will be searching for primary qualitative papers. The specific type of qualitative paper (i.e. phenomenological, ethnographic or grounded theory among others) will depend on your specific qualitative review question. Tables 4.3, 4.4 and 4.5 illustrate how the three different examples can be presented. These can be presented in tables or in narrative format as you prefer.

Specifying the types of participants to be included and excluded

To explain this process let's begin by discussing Cheryl's case study. Cheryl plans to include only children and adolescents aged 10 years of age or older when diagnosed. She makes it clear that the primary research papers she needs to find will include only those related to adolescents or children. She is also specifying that the age limit for including children will be either until they stop growing (as measured by pelvis or wrist radiographs or both) or until they are 18 years old.

Table 4.3   Cheryl's example for her scoliosis review (quantitative intervention study)

Type of studies	Include	Exclude
Quantitative	RCTs Clinical controlled trials Cohort	Commentaries Review documents Case studies Qualitative studies

Table 4.4   Mary's example for her domestic violence review (quantitative intervention study)

Type of studies	Include	Exclude
Quantitative	RCTs Clinical controlled trials Cohort	Commentaries Review documents Case studies Qualitative studies

Table 4.5   Sue's example for her witnessed resuscitation review (qualitative study)

Type of studies	Include	Exclude
Qualitative	Phenomenological, grounded theory, descriptive, ethnography	Letters Commentaries Reviews Discussion papers Quantitative studies

Cheryl needs to be specific as to the types of patients she will be excluding. She has decided to exclude any patients where scoliosis was not the primary diagnosis, such as congenital, neurological, metabolic and post-traumatic. Cheryl's example can be seen in Table 4.6.

Let us now consider Sue's case study on witnessed resuscitation. Sue plans to include adult patients over the age of 18 years' up to 60 years of age. She thinks that patients younger or older than this age range may have perceptions that are quite different. Sue needs to provide the operational definition again, which in her case is 'resuscitation or invasive procedures' as well as the setting which will be 'within a tertiary setting (hospital)'. She also specifies the type of injury 'after suffering cardiac arrest or substantial injury warranting a lifesaving intervention'.

Finally, as Sue will be looking into the perspectives of three different populations – that is the patient, the family members and the healthcare professionals – she needs to specify who these will be. Family members include spouse, partner, close friend, carer,

Table 4.6 Cheryl's example for writing down the population criteria for her scoliosis review

	Inclusion criteria	*Exclusion criteria*
Clinical population and diagnosis	**State who the population will be and provide an operational definition**	**Specify what types of diagnosis will be excluded**
	Patients with adolescent idiopathic scoliosis (i.e. patients who develop a curve and rib hump when they are 10 years of age or older and for which there is no known cause)	Adults with idiopathic or degenerative scoliosis and adolescents with any type of secondary scoliosis (e.g. neurological, metabolic, post-traumatic)
Age	**Provide the upper and lower age limits with a rationale**	
	Age 10–18 or until the end of bone growth and measured by an X-ray of the wrist or pelvis	Children under 10, adults over 18 years of age and adolescents whose bone growth has ended
Stage or severity of disease	**In some clinical conditions it is important to know how long they have had the disease as the symptoms are likely to be more severe**	
	All curve types and magnitudes	Curves >50°
Other factors relevant to your population group	**Include any factors that it is important for the reader to know**	
	As defined by the Scoliosis Research Society (2006)	

parent, sibling, son and daughter. Healthcare professionals include any named nurse, charge nurse, nurse practitioner or sister whose role is advocating for the patient and who is part of the resuscitation team or is involved with the patient and family in the capacity of delivering a 'duty of care'. Other professionals include the consultant, specialist, doctor, surgeon, physiotherapist, social worker or occupational therapist. In Table 4.7 Sue includes three different populations to evaluate if there are differences in perceptions among them. In Table 4.8 Mary records the population criteria for her review.

In summary, when describing the inclusion and exclusion criteria for your population(s), it is important that you clearly state who the population(s) will be, specify their diagnosis, the severity and duration of the disease, who will be included as well as any other relevant factors as discussed above.

Table 4.7   Sue's example for writing down the three population criteria for her witnessed resuscitation review

	Inclusion criteria	Exclusion criteria
Population 1 *Patient*	Adult patients >18 years undergoing cardiopulmonary resuscitation/invasive procedure	No children <18 years, patients undergoing chemotherapy, patients suffering from chronic illness or who have a DNAR (do not attempt resuscitation). No lay person, onlooker, hospital porter, ward clerk
Population 2 *Family members*	Spouse, partner, close friend, carer, parent, sibling, son, daughter	Bystanders, friends
Population 3 *Healthcare profes-sionals*	Named nurse, charge nurse, nurse practitioner, sister, consultant, specialist, doctor, surgeon, physiotherapist, social worker, occupational therapist	Ward clerk, porters, housekeepers, priest

Table 4.8   Mary's example for writing down the population criteria for her domestic violence review

	Inclusion criteria	Exclusion criteria
Population	Women Adults >18 Experiencing or have experienced domestic violence in the past	Men, children and teenagers Women in lesbian relationships Women with disabilities Pregnant women

---

Practice session 4.2

Use the template in Box 4.2 for writing down the population criteria for your own review.

	Inclusion criteria	Exclusion criteria
Box 4.2 Template for recording your own population criteria		
Clinical population	*(State who the population will be and provide an operational definition)*	
Diagnosis	*(State and define the diagnosis)*	
Age	*(Provide the upper and lower age limits with a rationale)*	
Stage or severity of disease	*(In some clinical conditions, it is important to know how long patients have had the disease as the symptoms are likely to be more severe)*	
Other factors relevant to your population group	*(These can include any other factors that you think are important to include)*	

Specifying the interventions (or exposure) to be included and excluded

You could start this section by first describing the interventions you plan to evaluate for your review. Cheryl's example is shown in Table 4.9.

With regards to Mary's review on domestic violence, she provides a brief explanation of what is meant by 'community advocacy programmes' and then states which different types of programmes she will be including. In this section it would also be useful for her to state clearly whether the papers she is planning to use will include all types of programmes or only those with particular characteristics, for example only those that are run by women who have themselves experienced domestic violence

Table 4.9 An example of Cheryl's intervention criteria

	Inclusion criteria	*Exclusion criteria*
Intervention	All types of rigid, semi-rigid and elastic braces, worn for a specific number of hours, for a specific number of years	Electrotherapy Traction Exercise only
Comparative intervention	All possible control interventions and comparisons were included	None

Table 4.10 An example of Mary's intervention criteria

	Inclusion criteria	*Exclusion criteria*
Intervention	Advocacy (conducted within or outside of health setting) Community programmes (need to include a clear definition of these)	Not formal cognitive behavioural therapy
Comparative intervention	Usual general practitioner (GP) treatment (usually this means no treatment for domestic violence)	Other interventions Alternative therapies

and not those run only by healthcare professionals. One way of presenting the inclusion and exclusion criteria for Mary's review on domestic violence is shown in Table 4.10.

Another point to consider is whether or not you are planning to include interventions carried out all over the world or just in the UK. The Cochrane Collaboration (2009) recommends finding all available studies from all over the world, but if your specific review question relates to treatment methods conducted within the UK, it is best to explain this and provide a rationale.

Sue's inclusion and exclusion criteria for her review on witnessed resuscitation are shown in Table 4.11; her inclusion criteria are very comprehensive.

Specifying the comparative interventions to be included and excluded

The comparative intervention needs to be specified if you are using the PICO format but not if you plan to use the PEO format. If you have a comparative intervention, you need to state the inclusion and exclusion criteria for the comparative intervention(s) you will be including within your review. The comparative interventions for the two quantitative studies can be seen in Tables 4.9 and 4.10.

Table 4.11 An example of Sue's inclusion and exclusion criteria

	Inclusion criteria	Exclusion criteria
Exposure Witnessed cardiopulmonary resuscitation after patient suffers a cardiac arrest OR Invasive procedures performed while undergoing resuscitation or as a lifesaving measure	Tertiary setting, such as hospital intensive care unit (ICU), paediatric intensive care unit (PICU), maternity departments, coronary care unit (CCU), high dependency unit (HDU), accident and emergency departments Patient's home, ambulance or community setting	Hospice setting Rehabilitation establishment

Specifying the outcomes to be included and excluded

By outcome measures we are usually referring to measurable outcomes or clinical changes in health (Khan et al. 2003). Outcomes include body structures and functions like pain and fatigue, activities as in functional abilities and participation or quality of life questionnaires as seen in Box 4.3.

Box 4.3   Types of outcome measures

You will need to state what type of outcome measures will be included; examples are listed below:

- body structures and functions – weight, pain, fatigue
- activities – functional abilities, dexterity
- participation – physical independence, quality of life
- process measures – compliance, strength
- others – rates of domestic violence
- if qualitative review – experiences of subjects.

Note that it is not enough to state that you will be measuring 'quality of life'. You also need to add what standardized assessment tools or validated measuring instruments will be included. It is pointless including scales that are not reliable and/or validated as their results might not be accurate. Box 4.4 shows how Cheryl could write out her outcome measures.

Box 4.4 Cheryl's outcome measures

Progression of scoliosis as measured by:

- The Cobb angle in degrees [the Cobb angle was devised by a surgeon (John Cobb) and measures the curvature of the spine]
- Number of patients who have progressed by more than five degrees Cobb

Quality of life and disability as measured by:

- Specific validated quality of life questionnaires such as SRS-22 (Asher et al. 2003), SF-36 (Lai et al. 2006), and BSSK (Weiss et al. 2006)

Back pain as measured by:

- Validated visual analogue scales (visual analogue scales provide a simple technique for measuring subjective experience: McCormack et al. 1988)
- Use of medication
- Adverse effects as measured in the identified papers will be reported

---

In Sue's example the 'outcomes' she will be looking at are the experiences, views or perceptions of her three different populations (Table 4.12). Mary's intervention review question (Table 4.13) is similar to Cheryl's intervention review question.

Table 4.12 Sue's criteria for considering studies in her review based on the PEO structure

Outcomes	Inclusion criteria	Exclusion criteria
Psychological issues, experience, perception, views, feelings	Experiences, perceptions, views from all members of the population groups toward resuscitation and invasive procedures	Physical effects: insomnia, tachycardia, guilt

Table 4.13 Mary's criteria for considering studies in her review based on the PICO structure

Outcomes	Inclusion criteria	Exclusion criteria
Quantitative	Validated quality of life (QOL) scales (need to specify which ones)	Qualitative experiences

---

Practice session 4.3

For your own review question, select the appropriate template (PICO or PEO) and write out the inclusion and exclusion criteria for all the PICO (Box 4.5) or PEO (Box 4.6) components.

Box 4.5 PICO template to use for your own inclusion and exclusion criteria

	Inclusion criteria	*Exclusion criteria*
Population		
Intervention		
Comparative groups		
Outcome		
Type of studies		

Box 4.6   PEO template to use for your own inclusion and exclusion criteria

	Inclusion criteria	Exclusion criteria
Population		
Exposure		
Outcome		
Type of studies		

Key points

- A problem statement is a simple statement of 'what is'.
- The review question follows from the problem statement.
- The 'aim' of a project is to solve the problem and answer the review question.
- The 'objective' is usually more specific then the aim.
- The objectives state what the researcher is going to do.
- Your aims and objectives need to be written clearly and concisely.
- Always make sure you can identify the PICO or PEO elements within them.
- When writing your objectives think of what it is you will actually be doing.
- Ensure that your aims, objectives, research question and title are all saying the same thing. The best way of doing this is to use virtually the same words for all three.
- A high-quality systematic literature review should have inclusion and exclusion criteria that are reported before the review is conducted.
- It is important that your search can target the papers that will answer your question and exclude any irrelevant ones.
- The inclusion and exclusion criteria for your review need to be explicit and applied stringently.

Summary

This chapter discussed the meanings of and differences between a problem statement, a review question, aims and objectives. Methods of specifying the inclusion and exclusion criteria for the types of studies, the population(s), intervention, comparative intervention(s) or exposures and outcome measures were discussed and examples provided for quantitative and qualitative review questions. Templates were provided to help you write out your own problem statement, aims and objectives and your inclusion and exclusion criteria.

5 Conducting a comprehensive and systematic literature search

Overview

- Importance of undertaking a comprehensive and systematic search
- Aims of undertaking a comprehensive and systematic search
- Key factors to be considered when undertaking a comprehensive search
- Steps involved in converting your review question into a comprehensive search strategy

Importance of undertaking a comprehensive and systematic search

When you conduct a systematic review, it is important that you try to retrieve all studies (or as many as possible) relating to the specific question that your review is addressing. This means searching as widely as possible from a whole range of sources. Although you may eventually exclude some papers (if they do not meet all your inclusion criteria) it is important that all the relevant studies are found and considered to ensure that your sample (all the studies you include) is as unbiased as possible. It is usually necessary to search a wide variety of databases and internet search engines as well as hand searching, which 'involves a manual page-by-page examination of the entire contents of a journal issue to identify all eligible reports of trials, whether they appear in articles, abstracts, news columns, editorials, letters or other text' (Higgins and Deeks 2009).

Aims of undertaking a comprehensive and systematic search

The aim of the search is to generate a comprehensive list of primary studies, both published and unpublished, which may be suitable for answering the proposed research question. The validity (truthfulness) of the review is directly related to the thoroughness of the search and its ability to identify all the relevant studies (Centre for Reviews and Dissemination 2008). Conducting a comprehensive literature search also helps to identify current knowledge with regard to relevant concepts and contexts and what is known and unknown in a particular field (Petticrew and Roberts 2006).

A comprehensive search strategy underlies the quality of the literature search, which in turn underlies the quality of the findings for the systematic review (Alderson and Green 2002). Any conclusions made following the review are only as good as the range and quality of the literature obtained.

It is important to search widely and thoroughly because not all research is published in journals. Additionally, not all the research published in journals is indexed in major databases and may not be easily retrievable (Bruce et al. 2008). Other reasons for searching widely include the fact that there may be a long wait before publication. Publication gaps after conference presentations are common because it takes authors a considerable amount of time to write up their findings, submit them, get them reviewed and then amended as necessary. Discovering a conference paper before publication could be important as it will provide some, although limited, information.

Problems with searching include publication and language bias (Dickersin et al. 2002). Publication bias means that positive results tend to be published more frequently than negative results in journals (Bruce et al. 2008). Language bias refers to the fact that positive results are more likely to be published in English. Egger et al. (1997) found that researchers who obtained statistically significant results in RCTs were more likely to publish in an English-language journal. Researchers and students are more likely to read research in their own language.

Bias may also relate to the geographical coverage of journals and databases. Some journals and databases tend to publish articles originating primarily from certain countries. The MEDLINE database, for example, includes approximately 10 million references, half (52 per cent) of which originate from the United States alone (Bruce et al. 2008).

Key factors to be considered when undertaking a comprehensive search

A number of key factors should be considered when undertaking a search for relevant articles, including the following:

- Reading reference lists will identify source ideas and concepts that highlight the design of studies.
- Hand searching may help to avoid possible bias in 'keyword' search systems. Keyword search systems like MEDLINE help reviewers to identify published studies more easily. However, Armstrong et al. (2005) state:

> information technology and the processes associated with indexing are not infallible. Studies may not be correctly marked by study design

which may mean they are missed in the electronic searching process. Handsearching for evidence of intervention effectiveness has therefore become a recognized tool in the systematic review process.

(Armstrong et al. 2005: 388)

- Accessing 'grey' literature, for example conference proceedings and PhD theses, will provide smaller and unpublished studies which may still be robust enough to provide valuable information.
- Getting in touch with authors of key articles may lead to them providing access to some of their important but unpublished work.

Steps involved in converting your review question into a comprehensive search strategy

There are a number of steps involved in converting the review question into a search strategy. The first step is to refer back to the keywords that will form the basis of the search. Timmins and McCabe (2005: 44) stated that 'The use of appropriate keywords is the cornerstone of an effective search'. It is possible to conduct searches using both index terms and free text searching. Index terms include terms used by electronic databases, which may not precisely match the terms in the research question, for example the MeSH (Medical Subject Headings) database in MEDLINE. To ensure that a search is comprehensive and both sensitive and specific, free text searching, also known as 'natural language' or language we use daily, should be used in addition to or instead of index term searching (Lahlafi 2007). This section provides an overview of all the steps involved in conducting a comprehensive search for a systematic literature review in nursing practice. This includes a discussion of the whole process and will be illustrated by the three case studies introduced in previous chapters.

Step 1: write out the research question and identify the component parts

As mentioned in Chapter 2, the first step is to write out the research question and identify the PICO (population, intervention, comparative intervention, outcomes) or PEO (population, exposure, outcomes) components. Templates are provided for both the PICO and PEO types of questions below. Referring back to two of the case studies (Mary and Cheryl), these can be written out as shown in Tables 5.1 and 5.2.

Table 5.1 Key components of Mary's intervention research question on domestic violence based on the PICO structure

P	I	C	O
Women who have experienced domestic violence	Advocacy programmes	General practice or routine treatment	Quantitative quality of life (measured by the SF-36 scale)

Table 5.2 Key components of Cheryl's intervention research question on adolescent idiopathic scoliosis based on the PICO structure

P	I	C	O
Patients with adolescent idiopathic scoliosis	how effective is bracing	as compared to observation	at reducing spinal curvature, rib hump and psychological problems?

Practice session 5.1

Once you have read the above examples, use one of the empty templates below based on the PICO and PEO structures to write out the components of your own review question (Boxes 5.1 and 5.2). You could add another column T if you wish to include the *type* of studies you will be including.

Box 5.1 PICO template to use for your own review question

P	I	C	O

Step 2: identify any synonyms

The second step is to identify any synonyms (words that mean the same thing) for all the component parts (P, I, C, O or P, E, O) of the review question. For example, other terms for 'scoliosis' are 'curvature of the spine', or 'spinal deformity'. It is essential to understand that any search needs to be both sensitive and specific. Sensitivity (in this context) refers to a search that picks up all the research articles that are potentially relevant. Specificity refers to a search that selects only those research articles that are directly relevant.

It is important to identify all the synonyms relating to the question and then to combine them using specific words called Boolean operators: these are words used in

Box 5.2 PEO template to use for your own review question		
P	E	O

searches to combine different keywords or phrases. A list of the most common operators include the following:

- OR – finds citations containing either of the specified keywords or phrases (sensitivity).
- AND – finds citations containing all of the specified keywords or phrases (specificity).
- NOT – excludes citations containing specified keywords or phrases.

The various steps will be identified using the case studies involving Mary and Cheryl.

Mary's case study: identifying synonyms and combining keywords

Mary is researching domestic violence and needs to identify synonyms for all the PICO components of her research question (Table 5.3). She was having difficulty thinking of synonyms, so she decides to use a thesaurus. To help her in this task she uses a template (Table 5.4). This template has a column for each letter of PICO (these can also be called strings) and a row for each synonym.

Using this type of template enables Mary to combine all the related terms of her question to try to obtain as many relevant articles as possible. It also optimizes the sensitivity and specificity of her search. In order to explain this further let's refer back

Table 5.3 Mary's research question in the PICO format

P	I	C	O
Women who have experienced domestic violence	Advocacy programmes	General practice or routine treatment	Quantitative quality of life (measured by the SF-36 scale)

Table 5.4 Empty template used by Mary to identify the synonyms for her review question and help her combine her keywords

Column terms combined with	Patient/condition AND	Intervention AND	Comparative intervention AND	Outcomes AND
OR				
OR				
OR				
OR				

to her question above. If we start with the population column P, Mary first needs to find synonyms for 'women who have experienced domestic violence'. Synonyms for this could include 'wife abuse', 'partner abuse', 'battered women' and 'spouse abuse'.

In Table 5.5, Mary first creates a list under the heading of Patient/condition with each synonym in a new row and numbers them from 1 to 9 (there just happen to be nine in this particular case).

The numbers represent the order or the individual steps of how the words will be typed into the search database (e.g. EBSCO or CINAHL) and have been included to help you understand how this process is conducted. This is repeated for the intervention 'I' (steps 11–19), the comparative intervention 'C' (steps 21–26) and the outcomes 'O' (step 28). When all the words in each of the four columns have been combined with 'OR', all the synonyms for P, I, C and O are combined using the Boolean term 'AND'. Thus the final part of the search strategy is to combine steps 10+20+27+28 together using the Boolean term 'AND'. I know this sounds very complicated but once you have followed the three examples below, the process should be much clearer.

Table 5.5 Mary's completed template used to identify the synonyms for her review question and help her combine her keywords

Column terms combined with	Patient/condition AND	Intervention AND	Comparative intervention AND	Outcomes AND
OR	1 Domestic violence	11 Treatment	21 General practice	28 Women's quality of life
OR	2 Wife abuse	12 Group support	22 GP	
OR	3 Partner abuse	13 Individual support	23 Routine treatment	
OR	4 Battered women	14 Advocacy programme	24 Doctor	
OR	5 Spouse abuse	15 Counselling	25 Physician	
OR	6 Rape	16 Community	26 Surgery	
OR	7 Sexual abuse	17 Therapy		
OR	8 Coercion	18 Support		
OR	9 Murder	19 Advocacy		
	10 Combine 1–9 using 'OR'	20 Combine 11–19 using 'OR'	27 Combine 21–26 using 'OR'	28

The last step is to combine steps 10+20+27+28 together using the term 'AND'

Step 3: identify truncations and abbreviations

Once you have identified your synonyms, the third step is to identify any truncations or abbreviations. The symbol $ is a shortcut termed 'truncation' and identifies variations of a word. What this means is if Mary, for example, searched using the word 'therapy', the search would only look for the word 'therapy' and leave out anything like therapeutic, therapist, therapists, etc. In some databases you may find that the truncation is indicated with a star * at the end of the word. Please make sure that you read all the relevant information specific to the database before you use it to ensure that you are using the correct truncation sign. If in any doubt consult with a librarian.

Mary was finding this part a little hard so she looked at other reviews on a similar topic and also used a hard copy thesaurus (these tend to be much more comprehensive than online ones) and a dictionary to help her. Going back to Mary's example, her truncations can be seen in Table 5.6 ($ dollar sign). If you find this part quite hard there is no need to worry. This step is not absolutely necessary because you can also conduct the search using the full terms: it will just take a bit longer.

Sometimes it is also necessary to identify abbreviations that are commonly used. For example, the intervention 'cognitive behavioural therapy', is frequently found as CBT in the literature.

Cheryl's case study: identifying synonyms

As with Mary's case study, Cheryl begins by identifying the key components of her review question (Table 5.7) and then starts identifying the synonyms to her keywords.

Cheryl's population group are patients with adolescent idiopathic scoliosis. She writes this under the population heading (column) and numbers it 1. What other synonyms are there for AIS? She could use the terms 'spinal deformity' (2), 'spinal curvature' (3), 'lateral curvature' (4), 'crooked spine' (5), 'rib hump' (6) and 'poor posture' (7), which now all need to be numbered in sequence from 2 to 7.

Table 5.6 An example of how Mary could identify truncations for her key terms

Column terms combined with	Patient/condition AND	Intervention AND	Comparative intervention AND	Outcomes AND
OR	1 Domestic violence	11 Treat$	21 General practice	28 Women's quality of life
OR	2 Wife abuse	12 Group support	22 GP	
OR	3 Partner abuse	13 Individual support	23 Routine treatment	
OR	4 Battered wom$	14 Advocacy program$	24 Doctor$	
OR	5 Spouse abuse	15 Counsel$	25 Physician$	
OR	6 Rape	16 Community	26 Surger$	
OR	7 Sexual abuse	17 Therap$		
OR	8 Coerc$	18 Support		
OR	9 Murder	19 Advocacy		
	10 Combine 1–9 using 'OR'	20 Combine 11–19 using 'OR'	27 Combine 21–26 using 'OR'	28

The last step is to combine steps 10+20+27+28 together using the term 'AND'

Table 5.7 Key components of Cheryl's intervention research question on adolescent idiopathic scoliosis based on the PICO structure

P	I	C	O
Patients with adolescent idiopathic scoliosis	how effective is bracing	as compared to observation	at reducing spinal curvature, rib hump and psychological problems?

Cheryl now needs to combine all the synonyms using the Boolean operator 'OR' (Table 5.8). This simply means that she is asking the search engine to search for any papers that have as a population group any of the synonyms listed. So this will be step 8 and can be written as [combine 1–7 using 'OR']. In other words she is trying to make her search as sensitive as possible. The Boolean operator 'OR' finds citations containing any of the specified keywords, phrases or synonyms (sensitivity).

Cheryl's next step is to repeat this process for the intervention, comparative interventions and outcomes columns on the template. The word 'brace' under the intervention heading will now be step 9, the word 'rigid brace' will now be step 10, 'semi-rigid brace' step 11, 'soft brace' step 12 and 'spinal orthosis' step 13. Cheryl cannot think of any more synonyms and cannot find any more in the thesaurus, so she now needs to let the search engine know that she would like to look for any of the listed synonyms for the word 'brace'. Cheryl will now write this as follows: step 16 [combine 9–15 using 'OR'] and will write them in the intervention column below (Table 5.8) (please refer to page 76 for Cheryl's full search strategy list).

Cheryl continues doing this for the comparative intervention column and the outcomes. The last step is for her to combine all the 'OR' combinations for each column (8+16+24+33) using the Boolean operator 'AND', which will find citations containing all of the specified keywords or phrases (specificity). To summarize, this will enable Cheryl to make her search as sensitive and specific as possible in order to enable her to find as many relevant citations as possible to answer her review question.

Table 5.8 Template used by Cheryl to start identifying keyword synonyms

Column terms combined with	Patient/condition AND	Intervention AND	Comparative intervention AND	Outcomes AND
OR	1 Patients with adolescent idiopathic scoliosis (AIS)			
OR	2 Spinal deformity			
OR	3 Spinal curvature			
OR	4 Lateral curvature			
OR	5 Crooked spine			
OR	6 Rib hump			
OR	7 Poor posture			
	8 Combine 1–7 using 'OR'			

Practice session 5.2

Now that we have discussed two examples, try to identify the synonyms and truncations for the review question you developed in Chapter 2 and then try to combine the keywords by using one of the templates provided. There are templates for both PICO and PEO formats.

Box 5.3   PICO template to use for your own review question to identify synonyms and combine keywords

Column terms combined with	Patient/ condition AND	Intervention AND	Comparative intervention AND	Outcomes AND
OR				
OR				
OR				
OR				

Box 5.4   PEO template to use for your own review question to identify synonyms and combine keywords

Column terms combined with	Patient/ condition AND	Exposure AND	Outcomes AND
OR			
OR			
OR			
OR			

Step 4: develop a search strategy string

The fourth step is to develop a search strategy string (i.e. a list of words) to input into the different databases. Keywords and synonyms need to be 'translated' or 'tweaked' to develop a search strategy list. The following list shows exactly which words Mary will be typing into a specific database (e.g. EBSCO or CINAHL or MEDLINE) to conduct her search and the order and combinations of how she will type them in. Following on from the template above, Mary first types the words from 1 to 9 individually into the database search engine. Once she has done this she will need to combine them using the word 'OR' (line 10). This is repeated for the remaining columns – intervention I (20), comparative intervention C (27) and outcomes column O (28). Once she has done this, all the PICO synonyms need to be combined using the term 'AND' which means she will need to combine the numbers 10, 20, 27 and 28. Mary's sequence for doing this is shown below:

1   Domestic violence
2   Wife abuse
3   Partner abuse
4   Battered women
5   Spouse abuse
6   Rape
7   Sexual abuse
8   Coercion
9   Murder
10   1 OR 2 OR 3 OR 4 OR 5 OR 6 OR 7 OR 8 OR 9 (Mary has combined terms using 'OR')
11   Treatment
12   Group support
13   Individual support
14   Advocacy programme
15   Counselling
16   Community
17   Therapy
18   Support
19   Advocacy
20   11 OR 12 OR 13 OR 14 OR 15 OR 16 OR 17 OR 18 OR 19 (Mary has combined terms using 'OR')
21   General practice
22   GP
23   Routine treatment
24   Doctor
25   Physician
26   Surgery
27   21 OR 22 OR 23 OR 24 OR 25 OR 26 (Mary has combined terms using 'OR')
28   Quality of life
29   10 AND 20 AND 27 AND 28 (Mary has combined the terms using 'AND').

It is preferable to apply limits at the final stage of the literature search. Limits can include restricting the search to English-language articles, human studies, research articles and possibly specifying a date range (you will need to provide a rationale for this, it shouldn't just be arbitrary). For example, if there had been a significant change in advocacy programmes since 1990, it would be wise to limit the search strategy to articles written after this date. Different limits are available in different databases. If limiting a search to English-language articles only, it is important to acknowledge that a language bias has been introduced into the search as you may have left out potentially important and relevant articles written in other languages. Cheryl's strategy list example can be found below:

1   Patients with adolescent idiopathic scoliosis
2   Spinal deformity
3   Spinal curvature
4   Lateral curvature
5   Crooked spine
6   Rib hump
7   Poor posture
8   Combine 1–7 using 'OR'
9   Brace$
10 Rigid brace$
11 Semi-rigid brace$
12 Soft brace$
13 Spinal orthosis
14 Orthopaedic device$
15 Orthopaedic equipment
16 Combine 9–15 using 'OR'
17 Exercise$
18 Brace$
19 Semi-rigid brace$
20 Rigid brace$
21 Electrical stimulation
22 Orthopaedic devices
23 Orthopaedic equipment
24 Combine 17–23 using 'OR'
25 Spinal curvature$
26 Rib hump$
27 Posture$
28 Back shape
29 Self-esteem
30 Self-confidence
31 Quality of life
32 Pain
33 Combine 25–32 using 'OR'
34 Combine 8 AND 16 AND 24 AND 33.

Practice session 5.3

With your own review question in mind, use the template in Box 5.5 to translate all the keywords and synonyms into a search strategy list like the ones developed by Mary and Cheryl.

Box 5.5   Template to use for translating your review question keywords into a search strategy list

1
2
3
4
5
6
7
8
9
10
11
12
13
14
15
16
17
18
19
20
21
22
23
24
25
26
27
28
29
30

Step 5: undertake a comprehensive search using all possible sources of information

The fifth step, having completed your search strategy string, is to undertake a comprehensive search, using databases and all other sources of information that are most relevant to your review question. Sources of information fall into several categories including online general databases, specialist databases, journal articles, grey literature, subject gateways, conference papers and proceedings, dissertation abstracts, contacting experts (clinical and non-clinical) and books. Below is a brief description of each type of information source together with its weblink.

General databases

Online databases include general databases like CINAHL, MEDLINE and AMED. An excellent publication called 'Finding studies for systematic reviews: a checklist for researchers' is available on the Centre for Reviews and Dissemination website at www.york.ac.uk/inst/crd/finding_studies_systematic_reviews.htm [accessed 31 August 2011]. This website includes a comprehensive list of the websites and other sources of information a reviewer should search when conducting a comprehensive search. Some online health databases are listed in Box 5.6.

Box 5.6   Websites for some online health databases

- MEDLINE
  www.nlm.nih.gov/bsd/pmresources.html
  MEDLINE is the main source for bibliographic coverage of biomedical literature; it covers 4600 journals from 1950 to the present.
- CINAHL
  www.ebscohost.com/cinahl
  The Cumulative Index to Nursing and Allied Health Literature (CINAHL) is a comprehensive and authoritative resource for the professional literature of nursing, allied health, biomedicine and healthcare.
- PsycINFO
  www.apa.org/pubs/databases/psycinfo/index.aspx
  The American Psychological Association's PsycINFO database records professional and academic literature in psychology and related disciplines, including medicine, psychiatry, nursing, sociology, pharmacology, physiology and linguistics.
- AMED
  www.bl.uk/reshelp/findhelpsubject/scitectenv/medicinehealth/amed/amed.html
  The Allied and Complementary Medicine Database (AMED) covers a selection of journals related to physiotherapy, occupational therapy, palliative care and complementary medicine.
- ASSIA
  www.csa.com/factsheets/assia-set-c.php

The Applied Social Sciences Index and Abstracts (ASSIA) website provides a comprehensive source of social science and health information for the practical and academic professional.
- REHABDATA
  www.naric.com/research/rehab
  The National Rehabilitation Information Center (NARIC) produces the REHABDATA database, providing information on physical, mental and psychiatric disabilities, independent living, vocational rehabilitation, special education, employment and assistive technology.
- Evidence-Based Medicine Reviews (EBMR)
  www.ovid.com/site/catalog/DataBase/904.jsp
  EBMR contains a number of links, including Cochrane Database of Systematic Reviews (CDSR), Database of Abstracts of Reviews of Effectiveness (DARE), American College of Physicians (ACP) Journal Club and Cochrane Controlled Trials Register (CCTR).

Specialist databases
There are many online specialist databases covering particular medical specialties. For example, the National Cancer Institute website can be found at www.cancer.gov/cancertopics/pdq/cancerdatabase

Journal articles
Journal articles are primary sources. These are the most up-to-date sources of peer-reviewed journals and information on advances and developments in treatment or care (most of the searches above will direct you to primary research papers).

Grey literature
Grey literature or non-journal literature refers to any unpublished sources of evidence. Most of the searches above focus on journal literature, but there are high rates of non-publication of research papers and many PhD theses are not published, therefore it is essential to search the grey literature. Grey literature also refers to published abstracts, conference proceedings, policy documents, newsletters and other unpublished written material. OpenGrey (System for Information on Grey Literature) is an open access website (www.opengrey.eu/) that has up to 700,000 bibliographical references of grey literature (paper) produced in Europe. OpenGrey covers science, technology, biomedical science, economics, social science and humanities.

Subject gateways
Subject gateways provide access to reliable and up-to-date web resources for all subjects, which have been carefully chosen and quality checked by experts in their field. Subject gateways are also called subject guides, subject directories and subject portals. They allow you to browse subject lists of good quality and evaluated subject resources. Some of the more important nursing and general health-related subject gateways are listed in Box 5.7.

Box 5.7   Websites for some nursing and general health-related subject gateways

---

- Nursing Portal
  www.nursing-portal.com
  The Nursing Portal is a gateway to the world of nursing.
- MentalHelp.net
  www.mentalhelp.net
  The MentalHelp.net website promotes mental health and wellness.
- National Library for Health
  www.evidence.nhs.uk/nhs-evidence-content/journals-and-databases
  The UK NHS Evidence website includes a national health library and information service.
- SearchMedica
  www.searchmedica.co.uk
  SearchMedica is an open access medical search engine.
- Social Care Online
  www.scie-socialcareonline.org.uk
  Social Care Online promotes better knowledge for better practice.
- Google and Google Scholar
  www.google.co.uk and scholar.google.co.uk
  Two of the best known general purpose search engines.

Conference papers and proceedings

Conference papers and proceedings include the ISI proceedings: science and technology edition. Contains details of approximately 10000 conferences per year. http://wok.mimas.ac.uk/

Dissertation abstracts

Dissertation abstracts can be found at http://library.dialog.com/bluesheets/html/bl0035.html or on a database called Index to Thesis, which contains dissertations from most of the universities in the United Kingdom: www.theses.com

Contacting experts (clinical and non-clinical)

The easiest way to contact experts and clinical and non-clinical specialists in your field of study is to google their name to find a research paper that they have written. Most papers include the email address of the authors.

Books

Books are useful secondary sources for identifying 'stable' sources of information and developing your background knowledge of a research problem. Information on books can be rather old. From the time the book is first written and then published, several years may have gone by.

Step 6: save your searches

The final step is to record and save any searches as well as the results of the searches in an electronic format, so that all the necessary information will be available and easily accessible when it comes to writing up the review. The search strategy, including the database, the title of the article, the abstract, the host, for example OVID or EBSCO, and the date should be logged (see example in Box 5.8). As much detail as possible should be recorded to enable a colleague or otherwise to replicate the review if needed. This makes your search strategy more valid and will be useful if the search needs to be carried out again at a later date. Discussion of the 'hits' obtained and the selection process used to identify articles for closer study will also provide an audit trail.

Box 5.8 Template example of how you could document your first search					
Database	*Dates covered*	*Date searched*	*Hits*	*Full record/titles and abstracts*	*Notes*
MEDLINE (EBSCO host)	1990–2012	20/03/12	23	*(Titles of the articles could be included here)*	*(You may want to give your search strategy a name, for example 'Medline1' just in case you need to run the search again sometime in the future)*

Below is one way you could write up the databases you have searched:

- Cumulative Index to Nursing and Allied Health Literature (CINAHL) (1982 to 12/2011)
- MEDLINE (1966 to 12/2011)
- British Nursing Index (BNI) (1994 to 12/2011)
- Allied and Complementary Medicine Database (AMED) (1985 to 12/2011)
- Proquest (1990 to 12/2011)
- PsycINFO (2000 to 12/2011)
- Scopus (1990 to 12/2011)
- Embase (1988 to 12/2011)
- Science Direct (1990 to 12/2011)
- PubMed (1995 to 12/2011)
- Internurse (1995 to 12/2011)
- Health Management Information Consortium (HMIC) (12/2011).

Practice session 5.4
Try to document the search strategy for your own research question, using the format in Box 5.9.

Box 5.9 Template to use for documenting your search strategy					
Database	Dates covered	Date searched	Hits	Full record/titles and abstracts	Notes

Key points

- The aim of a comprehensive and systematic search is to generate a comprehensive list of primary studies, both published and unpublished, which may be suitable for answering the proposed research question.
- Try to retrieve all studies (or as many as possible) pertaining to the specific question that your review is addressing, searching as widely as possible from a whole range of sources.
- It is necessary to search a wide variety of databases and internet search engines as well as hand searching and grey literature.
- Problems with searching include publication bias and language
- Publication bias means that positive results tend to be published more frequently than negative results in journals.
- Language bias refers to the fact that positive results are more likely to be published in English.
- Bias may also relate to the geographical coverage of journals and databases.
- Key activities include reading reference lists, hand searching, accessing grey literature and getting in touch with authors of key articles.
- There are six steps involved in converting the review question into a comprehensive search strategy.
- Step 1 is to write out the research question and identify the PICO (population, intervention, comparative intervention, outcomes) or PEO (population, exposure, outcomes) component parts.
- Step 2 is to identify any synonyms (words that mean the same thing) for all the component parts (P, I, C, O or P, E, O) of the review question.
- Step 3 is to identify truncations and abbreviations.
- Step 4 is to develop a search strategy string (list of words) to input into the different databases.
- Step 5 is to undertake your comprehensive search using all sources of information.
- Step 6 is to save your searches.

Summary

This chapter discussed the importance, the rationale and the aims of undertaking a comprehensive and systematic search. The chapter described the key factors to be considered when undertaking a comprehensive search. The six steps involved in converting your review question into a comprehensive search strategy were described in detail.

6 Working with your primary papers
Selecting, appraising and extracting data

Overview

- Selecting the appropriate papers to answer your review question
- Appraising the methodological quality of the research papers that you have selected
- Extracting the appropriate data from your research papers

Selecting the appropriate papers to answer your review question

Once you have conducted your search and specified your inclusion and exclusion criteria, the next step in conducting a systematic literature review is to select the studies that meet all your predetermined selection criteria. The actual process of how you select the studies to include in your review needs to be described in sufficient methodological detail to enable the steps to be replicated and thus ensure the whole process is transparent. This will enable the appropriateness of the methods used to be easily evaluated and duplicated. This part of the review aims to filter out any irrelevant articles (Torgerson 2003).

The process of selecting studies for inclusion or exclusion in the review consists of two phases; the first phase involves sifting through the titles and abstracts of all the articles retrieved from the search, screening them systematically and selecting those that meet the predetermined inclusion criteria. The second phase involves reading the full text of each identified article. For both phases it is useful to make an appropriate research paper selection form to help you standardize the way you select the articles that meet your predetermined criteria. This helps to make sure that you are always selecting the papers in the same way (i.e. it standardizes the process) and it also helps to improve the validity or truthfulness of the results. To explain how you make this form, let's look at examples from the three case studies on domestic violence (Mary), scoliosis (Cheryl) and witnessed resuscitation (Sue).

Let us first discuss how to make the paper selection form, using Mary's case study on domestic violence. Chapter 4 described how to specify your inclusion and exclusion criteria. To make your paper selection form, all you need to do is copy the inclusion criteria and then turn these criteria into questions.

Mary starts by finding the electronic copy of her inclusion and exclusion criteria and copies the first two columns – the column entitled PICO components and the inclusion criteria column. Mary then turns all her original listed inclusion criteria statements into questions (usually this can be as simple as adding a question mark) as can be seen in Tables 6.1 and 6.2.

She then adds another row to the bottom of her table to record the action with the rationale she will take and also adds another column to the right side of the table (the decision column) to enable her to write whether or not that specific title and abstract meet the criteria (see Table 6.2)

Table 6.1 An example of Mary's inclusion and exclusion criteria

PICO components	Inclusion criteria	Exclusion criteria
Population	Women Adults > 18 Experiencing or have experienced domestic violence in the past	Men, children and teenagers Women in lesbian relationships Women with disabilities Pregnant women
Intervention	Advocacy (conducted within or outside of health setting) Community programmes (need to include a clear definition of these)	Not formal cognitive behavioural therapy
Comparative intervention	Usual (GP) treatment (usually this means no treatment for domestic violence)	Other interventions Alternative therapies
Outcomes Quantitative	Validated quality of life scales (need to specify which ones)	Experiences only on domestic violence or on children only

Table 6.2 An example of how Mary could write her study selection form

Paper number:	Title	Authors		
PICO components	Inclusion criteria	Decision: Yes	No	Undecided
Population	Women Adults > 18? Experiencing or have experienced domestic violence in the past?			
Intervention	Advocacy (conducted within or outside of health setting)? Community programmes?			
Comparative intervention	Usual (GP) treatment (usually this means no treatment for domestic violence)?			
Outcomes	Quality of life?			
Action (with Rationale)	Include (read full article) Exclude or Undecided			

Mary's answers can be only one out of a possible three: yes, the paper meets these criteria and is denoted by (Y), no, the paper does not meet these criteria and is denoted by (N), or undecided as to whether this paper meets the inclusion criteria or not and is denoted by (U). If Mary is undecided, she will need to read the whole paper as well as ask a colleague or a supervisor for their opinion.

It is important to test your paper selection form on a couple of articles to make sure that it is good for purpose (this is similar to conducting a pilot study when doing primary research). Although it is perfectly possible to select your papers on your own, it is important to remember that it would strengthen the validity (truthfulness) of your results if you can ask a friend or colleague to select the papers independently to see if they obtain the same results (Petticrew and Roberts 2006; Torgerson 2003). If you cannot find anyone, you should just acknowledge this.

Sue decided to use a slightly different format for her form (Table 6.3). She has decided she wants to use one form to select a number of studies. Although she will use less paper, this format does have a few limitations. She will be restricted in the amount of detail that she can include on her form and she will need to add a key to the bottom of the form, to clarify which specific paper each number on the top row of the form represents. It may also be difficult for her to write any specific queries that may arise from assessing each of her criteria for all her papers.

After Sue has looked at three titles and abstracts, she fills in the first three columns on her selection form that represent these three papers (Table 6.3). In column 1 all the criteria have been met and Sue's overall decision (the action at the bottom) is to include the paper. In column 2 the action is to exclude the paper as two of the criteria have not

Table 6.3   Example of Sue's first selection of papers based on title and abstract only

Paper and abstract number:	1	2	3	4	5	6	7	8	9	10	11	12
Population												
Adult patients	Y	N	?									
Age >18												
OR												
Family members OR	Y	Y	Y									
Healthcare professionals	Y	Y	Y									
Exposure												
Witnessed cardiopulmonary resuscitation	Y	Y	?									
or invasive procedures												
Outcomes												
Patient's experience of exposure	Y	Y	Y									
Family members' experience of exposure	Y	Y	Y									
Healthcare professionals' experience of exposure	Y	Y	Y									
Type of study												
Qualitative research	Y	N	Y									
*Action	Y	N	U									

*Action – Rationale: Y – Yes: fits criteria; N – No: does not fit criteria; U – Unsure: read paper.

been met. In column 3 there are two question marks, which means that Sue is undecided and needs to read the full paper and repeat the process. If she is still undecided after reading the full paper, she will need to consult with a colleague or supervisor. In summary the first phase can result in including an article, rejecting it or being undecided (Higgins and Deeks 2009).

Once Sue has finished the first part of the selection process, she will have a pile of abstracts that she has definitely decided to include, another pile about which she is uncertain and a third pile of abstracts that she has rejected. The first two piles must now be examined more closely for the second phase. This means obtaining full copies of the papers, reading them and making a decision regarding whether they meet the inclusion criteria that have been preset (Higgins and Deeks 2009).

Cheryl's paper selection form for selecting adolescent patients with idiopathic scoliosis is shown in Table 6.4.

Table 6.4 Cheryl's example for writing down the selection criteria for her review

		Decision		
Bibliographic details of paper	*Inclusion*	Y	N	U
Clinical population/diagnosis	• Patients with adolescent idiopathic scoliosis?			
Age	• Ages 10–18? • Or until the end of bone growth? • Measured by an X-ray of the wrist or pelvis?			
Intervention	• Rigid brace? • Semi-rigid brace? • Elastic brace? • Worn for how many hours per day? • How many days per week? • How many years?			
Comparative intervention	• Exercise? • Rigid brace? • Semi-rigid brace? • Soft brace? • Electrical stimulation? • Surgery?			
Outcomes	Progression of scoliosis as measured by: • Cobb angle in degrees? • Number of patients who have progressed by more than five degrees Cobb? Quality of life and disability as measured by? Specific validated quality of life questionnaires such as • SRS-22 (Asher et al. 2003)? • SF-36 (Lai et al. 2006)? • BSSK (Weiss et al. 2006)? Back pain as measured by: • Validated visual analogue scales? • Use of medication? • Adverse effects?			

Templates to select the papers for your own systematic literature review

Practice session 6.1
You have probably saved a number of papers from your searches and printed them out. Based on your own review question, select the appropriate template for either PICO (Box 6.1) or PEO (Box 6.2) (see pages 89 and 90) format to decide which of your primary research papers should be included, which should be excluded and which ones you are still undecided about. Once you have done this, you can go on to the next part of the study and appraise the methodological quality of your papers.

Box 6.1	PICO template to use for your own selection of papers			
Bibliographic details of paper (*Fill in the details of the paper you are evaluating here*)				
	Inclusion criteria	*Yes*	*No*	*Undecided*
Participants	(*This is where you write down the criteria for your population details, diagnosis, age etc.*)			
Intervention	(*Here you write down the specific criteria for your intervention*)			
Comparative intervention	(*Same but for comparative group*)			
Outcomes	(*Write down the specific outcomes you are looking for*)			
Type of study	*Write down the specific research designs you will be including*			
Action (with rationale)	*The action will be yes, no or undecided for the first phase and yes or no only for the second phase*			

Box 6.2 PEO template to use for your own selection of papers

Bibliographic details of paper

Abstract number	1	2	3	4	5	6	7
Population							
Exposure							
Outcomes							
Type of studies							
*Action							

*Action = Rationale:
Y – Yes: fits criteria
N – No: does not fit criteria
U – Undecided, read full paper

Appraising the methodological quality of the research papers that you have selected

Appraising 'study quality' is often used interchangeably with assessing the 'internal validity', which is the extent to which a study is free from methodological biases (Petticrew and Roberts 2006) or the degree to which the results of a study are likely to approximate the 'truth' (Higgins and Deeks 2009). In the context of systematic reviews, quality refers to the methodological quality – the internal and external validity of quantitative studies. Jadad (1998) suggested that the following points may be relevant when assessing the quality of randomized controlled trials:

- Relevance of the research question.
- Internal validity of the trial – the degree to which the trial design, conduct, analysis and presentation have minimized or avoided bias.
- External validity – the extent to which findings are generalizable.
- Appropriateness of the data analysis and presentation.
- Ethical implications of the intervention the paper evaluated. This refers to the ethics, for example was informed consent obtained, in the included papers within the review.

The criteria for qualitative articles are different. Qualitatives articles are often judged with regard to authenticity and trustworthiness, rather than validity or reliability (please see Figure 6.1 and guidelines below for a more detailed explanation). Table 6.5 shows the common features of research critique frameworks for both quantitative and qualitative studies.

Appraising the quality of articles is crucial as it allows the exploration of how differences in quality might explain differences in the study results, and it will also guide the interpretation of the findings and their value to practice. There are a number of practical issues to consider when appraising a study (Centre for Reviews and Dissemination

Table 6.5 Common features of research critique frameworks

Quantitative	Qualitative
Research design	Philosophical background
Experimental hypothesis	Research design
Operational definitions	Concepts
Population	Context
Sample	Sample
Sampling	Sampling
Validity/reliability of data collection	Auditability of data collection
Data analysis	Credibility/confirmability of data analysis
Generalizability	Transferability

Source: Reprinted from Caldwell, K., Henshaw, L. and Taylor, G. (2011) Developing a framework for critiquing health research: An early evaluation. *Nurse Education Today* 31(8): e1–7, with permission from Elsevier.

2008). These include stating who will be assessing the quality of the studies, how many reviewers will be involved, what checklist or scale will be used for quality assessment and how the reviewers will resolve disagreements. Involvement of a colleague or a supervisor is important (if possible) to ensure that all articles are appropriately critiqued.

The quality of evidence and conclusions generated by a systematic literature review for nursing practice depends entirely on the quality of the primary studies that make up the review. This quality assessment is one of the key features that sets apart a systematic review from a narrative review. To assess the quality of primary articles, a number of assessment tools are available that are easily accessible online (Box 6.3). It is important to use appropriate checklists or scales for the type of study design to be evaluated. Box 6.3 lists some of the scales that can be used to evaluate randomized and non-randomized studies, as well as websites where critical appraisal forms for different study designs can be found. There are literally hundreds of critical appraisal tools available in the literature.

Worked examples of both quantitative and qualitative critiques can be found in Chapters 4–6 of *The Evidence-Based Practice Manual for Nurses* (Craig and Smyth 2007).

Box 6.3   Websites for some common appraisal frameworks

- Critical Appraisal Skills Programme
  www.phru.nhs.uk/Pages/PHD/CASP.htm
- McMaster University *Evidence-Based Practice Research Group*
  www.srs-mcmaster.ca/Default.aspx?tabid=630
- Newcastle-Ottawa Scale (NOS) for assessing the quality of nonrandomized studies in meta-analysis
  www.ohri.ca/programs/clinical_epidemiology/oxford.htm

One set of critical appraisal forms that I often recommend to students is the McMaster framework for critiquing qualitative or quantitative studies (see Box 6.3). This framework includes excellent guidelines on how to conduct the different kinds of critical appraisals for both quantitative and qualitative research and provides advice for answering each of the questions. Although devised by occupational therapists, the framework is written in basic terms that can be understood by any clinician, researcher and student.

Another framework developed by Caldwell et al. (2011) for nursing students has combined both quantitative and qualitative appraisal questions into one form that can be used for any type of research design. Nursing students have found this framework (Figure 6.1) together with the guidelines both easy to use and to follow.

The framework by Caldwell et al. (2011) is supported by guidelines that provide an extended explanation of each item. It begins with questions that address both quantitative and qualitative studies:

- **Does the title reflect the content?**
  The title should be informative and indicate the focus of the study. It should

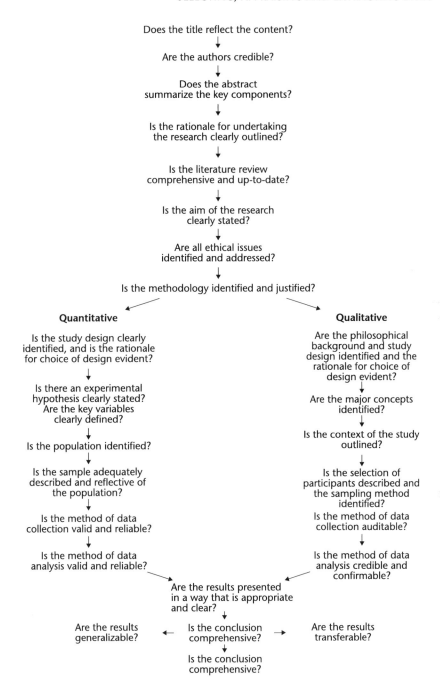

Figure 6.1 Framework and guidelines by Caldwell et al. (2011).

Source: Reprinted from Caldwell, K., Henshaw, L. and Taylor, G. (2011) Developing a framework for critiquing health research: An early evaluation. *Nurse Education Today* 31 (8): e1–7, with permission from Elsevier.

allow the reader to easily interpret the content of the study. An inaccurate or misleading title can confuse the reader.

- **Are the authors credible?**
  Researchers should hold appropriate academic qualifications and be linked to a professional field relevant to the research.

- **Does the abstract summarize the key components?**
  The abstract should provide a short summary of the study. It should include the aim of the study, outline of the methodology and the main findings. The purpose of the abstract is to allow the reader to decide if the study is of interest to them.

- **Is the rationale for undertaking the research clearly outlined?**
  The author should present a clear rationale for the research, setting it in context of any current issues and knowledge of the topic to date.

- **Is the literature review comprehensive and up-to-date?**
  The literature review should reflect the current state of knowledge relevant to the study and identify any gaps or conflicts. It should include key or classic studies on the topic as well as up-to-date literature. There should be a balance of primary and secondary sources.

- **Is the aim of the research clearly stated?**
  The aim of the study should be clearly stated and should convey what the researcher is setting out to achieve.

- **Are all ethical issues identified and addressed?**
  Ethical issues pertinent to the study should be discussed. The researcher should identify how the rights of informants have been protected and informed consent obtained. If the research is conducted within the National Health Service (NHS), there should be indication of local research ethics committee approval.

- **Is the methodology identified and justified?**
  The researcher should make clear which research strategy they are adopting, i.e. qualitative or quantitative. A clear rationale for the choice should also be provided, so that the reader can judge whether the chosen strategy is appropriate for the study. At this point the student is asked to look specifically at the questions that apply to the paradigm appropriate to the study they are critiquing.

- **Are the results presented in a way that is appropriate and clear?**
  Presentation of data should be clear, easily interpreted and consistent.

- **Is the discussion comprehensive?**
  In quantitative studies the results and discussion are presented separately. In qualitative studies these may be integrated. Whatever the mode of presentation, the researcher should compare and contrast the findings with that of previous research on the topic. The discussion should be balanced and avoid subjectivity.

- **Is the conclusion comprehensive?**
  Conclusions must be supported by the findings. The researcher should identify any limitations to the study. There may also be recommendations for further research or, if appropriate, implications for practice in the relevant field.

To complete your critique, the final questions that you need to address are applied to both quantitative and qualitative studies (see Table 6.6).

Table 6.6 Questions relevant to quantitative or qualitative research

Quantitative	Qualitative
Is the design clearly identified and a rationale provided? The design of the study, e.g. survey experiment, should be identified and justified. As with the choice of strategy, the reader needs to determine whether the design is appropriate for the research undertaken.	**Are the philosophical background and study design identified and the rationale for choice evident?** The design of the study, e.g. phenomenology, ethnography, should be identified and the philosophical background and rationale discussed. The reader needs to consider if it is appropriate to meet the aims of the study.
Is there an experimental hypothesis clearly stated and are the key variables identified? In experimental research, the researcher should provide a hypothesis. This should clearly identify the independent and dependent variables, and state their relationship and the intent of the study. In survey research the researcher may choose to provide a hypothesis, but it is not essential, and alternatively a research question or aim may be provided.	**Are the major concepts identified?** The researchers should make clear what the major concepts are, but they might not define them. The purpose of the study is to explore the concepts from the perspective of the participants.
Is the population identified? The population is the total number of units from which the researcher can gather data. It may be individuals, organizations or documentation. Whatever the unit, it must be clearly identified.	**Is the context of the study outlined?** The researcher should provide a description of the context of the study, how the study sites were determined and how the participants were selected.
Is the sample adequately described and reflective of the population? Both the method of sampling and the size of the sample should be stated so that the reader can judge whether the sample is representative of the population and sufficiently large to eliminate bias.	**Is the selection of the participants described and sampling method identified?** Informants are selected for their relevant knowledge or experience. Representativeness is not a criteria and purposive sampling is often used. Sample size may be determined through saturation.
Is the method of data collection valid and reliable? The process of data collection should be described. The tools or instruments must be appropriate to the aims of the study and the researcher should identify how reliability and validity were assured.	**Is the method of data collection auditable?** Data collection methods should be described, and be appropriate to the aims of the study. The researcher should describe how they assured that the method is auditable.
Is the method of data analysis valid and reliable? The method of data analysis must be described and justified. Any statistical test used should be appropriate for the data involved.	**Is the method of data analysis credible and confirmable?** The data analysis strategy should be identified; what processes were used to identify patterns and themes? The researcher should identify how credibility and confirmability have been addressed.

Source: Reprinted from Caldwell, K., Henshaw, L. and Taylor, G. (2011) Developing a framework for critiquing health research: An early evaluation. *Nurse Education Today* 31(8): e1–7, with permission from Elsevier.

Practice session 6.2

Once you have read through the framework and guidelines (Caldwell et al. 2011), work through the appropriate questions for your type of paper (qualitative or quantitative) and try to critique them. Alternatively, using their guidelines, you can select either the quantitative or the qualitative critical appraisal forms available on the McMaster site www.srs-mcmaster.ca/Default.aspx?tabid=630.

Extracting the appropriate data from your research papers

The data extraction phase is perhaps the most challenging aspect of the methodology. Data extraction involves going back to the primary articles and highlighting the relevant information that will answer the research question. Normally, this involves extracting data related to the population included, the intervention, comparative intervention and particularly the outcomes (the PICO components). To standardize this process and improve the validity of the results, it is crucial to compile a data extraction form. As with the selection form previously described, it is important to pilot the form on one or two of the articles to ensure it is useful and appropriate (Higgins and Deeks 2009).

Let us first consider Mary's quantitative case study example on domestic violence. Mary needs to look back at the PICO form she made when selecting her articles, presented earlier in this chapter. She knows that all the articles included in the final selection are relevant to the research question and have met the inclusion criteria. In the data extraction form, it is important that she extracts all the relevant information to enable her to answer her question related to women's quality of life. As well as collecting information on the population, intervention and control group, Mary will need to collect information on the outcomes. Table 6.7 provides an example of what one of Mary's data extraction forms might look like, together with my comments on what Mary needs to do in each section.

Turning to Sue's qualitative case study, Sue first needs to make a data extraction form as described above. This part of the process is identical whether you are planning to extract qualitative or quantitative data. The key difference between the two types of data extraction forms (qualitative or quantitative) is that the outcomes section in a qualitative data extraction form will be inserted under the main themes that were decided upon for your review question when you were planning your protocol or plan and the data extracted will be the 'words or perceptions' of the population group(s) you have decided to include. For quantitative data extraction forms, it is numbers that are mostly extracted.

Sue has decided to include three different population groups as listed in Box 6.4. When constructing the outcomes section of her data extraction form, she also included a section where she would write down the page number, column number and line numbers of the words extracted (sentences and paragraphs that she will extract from her papers). This will let her know what part of the paper the excerpt came from and improve the audit trail of her review. Table 6.8 provides an example of what Sue's data extraction form looked like before she filled it in.

Table 6.7   Example of Mary's data extraction form

Date of data extraction: 23/4/11 *(here Mary writes down the date when she fills in the form)*

Reviewer: Mary Smith *(here she writes her name as the reviewer of the paper)*

Bibliographic details of study: *(here she writes the reference for the paper)*

Jones, J. (2008) The effect of advocacy interventions compared to usual care on abused women's quality of life. *Journal of Clinical Nursing* 10,(5): 345–352.

Purpose of study: *(here she writes down the purpose of the paper from which she is extracting the data)*

The purpose of the study is to evaluate the effectiveness of a community advocacy programme as compared to usual care on abused women's quality of life.

Study design: *(here she writes down the study design – usually this can be found in the abstract)*

Randomized controlled trial

Population (sample): *(here she summarizes the information about the sample used in the paper)*

60 women who were or had previously experienced domestic violence were included in the study. The women were randomly allocated to either the intervention group (*n*=30) or the control group who received usual care (*n*=30).

Intervention: *(Mary summarizes what the intervention was)*

Women attended an advocacy group once a week over 12 weeks. Group meetings provided support and help for women on all aspects relevant to domestic violence.

Comparative intervention: *(the same for the comparative intervention)*

The women in this group received usual care.

Outcomes: *(This part is very important. Mary needs to search for the results of the study in the paper results section of the article. As her outcomes relate to quality of life scales she needs to copy the pre- and post-intervention values for both the advocacy group and the usual care group from each paper as seen below. In this case the results of this paper have been extracted.)*

> SF-36 quality of life scales
> Pre-intervention advocacy group 30/50 (50 is the average rate for healthy individuals)
> Post-intervention advocacy group 40/50
> Pre-intervention usual care group 29/50
> Post-intervention usual care group 30/50

Box 6.4   Sue's proposed outcomes

- Outcome 1: Patient's experience of resuscitation and/or invasive procedures.
- Outcome 2: Family members' experience of resuscitation and/or invasive procedures.
- Outcome 3: Healthcare professionals' experience of resuscitation and/or invasive procedures.

Table 6.8   Sample data extraction form

Date of data extraction:	*(Today's date)*
Reviewer:	*(Your name)*
Bibliographical details of study:	*(Full reference of article including author, year and source)*
Purpose of study:	*(This is outlined by the author of the article)*
Study design:	*(Type of qualitative study utilized for purpose of the article)*
Population (sample):	*(This section outlines the description of the study sample characteristics as identified)*
Number –	
Age –	
Ethnicity –	
Exposure:	*(Witnessed resuscitation and/or invasive procedures)*
Outcomes:	*(All outcomes of the population groups in question as below and measured in relation to the identified themes)*

OUTCOME 1

Patient's experience of resuscitation and/or invasive procedures

Page	Col.	Line	Data extracted	Sub-themes

OUTCOME 2

Family members' experience of resuscitation and/or invasive procedures

Page	Col.	Line	Data extracted	Sub-themes

OUTCOME 3

Healthcare professionals' experience of resuscitation and/or invasive procedures

Page	Col.	Line	Data extracted	Sub-themes

Once the data extraction form was ready, Sue was able to proceed with the data extraction process. There are a number of ways of extracting data from qualitative papers with no one way being dominant. The literature is somewhat controversial and vague within this area. Consequently, this has led to new researchers being unclear as to how precisely to proceed with extracting qualitative data. Below I have outlined one way of doing this but there are many different ways this can be done. The method described below has been adapted from Burnard's (1991) method of thematic analysis and follows the same methodology that you would use to analyse any qualitative data, for example interviews. Burnard (1991) has published an excellent detailed description of the steps involved in his article entitled 'A method of analysing interview transcripts in qualitative research'.

Step 1

Before Sue starts extracting qualitative data (i.e. words and sentences) it is important that she reads the results section of her primary papers a number of times to become fully immersed in the data. The purpose of immersion is to become more fully aware of the 'lived world' of the participants and to try to see the world from the other person's perspective.

Step 2

As part of her research question Sue has decided which specific themes she intends to look at as part of developing her review question. Sue is looking at the perspectives of three different population groups – the patients, the families and the healthcare professionals – and has colour coded them in three different colours. Sue's colour-coding scheme involves highlighting any perceptions in the primary research papers to do with patients in green, any families' perceptions in yellow and any healthcare professionals' perspectives in blue. This can be done either manually by using highlighter pens or electronically on the computer.

Step 3

The next step is to cut out (either manually or electronically) all the text highlighted in different colours and paste it in the 'Data extracted' section of the form. In Sue's scenario, all green highlighted text related to patients will be inserted under outcome 1 of the form, all yellow highlighted text related to family members will be inserted under outcome 2 of the form and the same for outcome 3. Eventually Sue will end up with all the data or text in the primary paper related to patients, family members and healthcare professionals (HCPs) under the appropriate headings and sections in the data extraction form (see Table 6.9). She also needs to make sure that she notes the page number, column number and line number from the primary paper as she will need this information when she refers to them in the results or discussion sections of her review. It is important to clarify your audit trail.

Step 4

In the data extraction form, Sue writes down as many headings as necessary to describe all aspects of the content excluding 'dross'. Field and Morse (1985) state that the term 'dross' is used to denote any unusable fillers in an interview or paper, such as issues that are unrelated to the topic in hand. The headings or category system should account for almost all the category data. This phase is known as *open coding*, meaning that categories are generated freely (Burnard 1991: 462).

Step 5

When Sue has written down all the categories for all the results section, the next step is for her to look through the headings and to try to group them together under 'higher order' headings. Burnard (1991) explains that the aim here is to reduce the number of categories by 'collapsing' some of the ones that are similar into broader categories. For example, it could be decided that all the headings in the 'categories' column could be collapsed into one higher order heading as shown in Table 6.9.

Step 6

The new list of categories are worked through and very similar headings are removed.

Step 7

This step is used to 'increase the validity of the categorizing method and to guard against researcher bias' (Burnard 1991: 463). It is important to ask one or two colleagues to independently generate the categories from the same research paper without looking at your own list. Once this has been done the categories are discussed and any changes made as necessary.

Table 6.9   Healthcare professionals' experience of resuscitation and/or invasive procedures

			Outcome/theme 3			
			Healthcare professionals' experience of resuscitaton and/or invasive procedures			*Higher order*
Page	*Col.*	*Line*	*Data extracted*	*Open coding*	*Categories*	*headings*
60	1	35–36	Other concerns stemmed from the insertion of chest drains, defibrillating, putting in tubes, inserting needles and intubation.	Concerns arising from insertion of diverse medical devices	HCP's concerns relating to family's needs	HCP's concerns for family needs and feelings during the procedure
61	1	1–3	All of these are invasive procedures that are	Invasive procedures	Invasive and abnormal procedures	
			'abnormal in their (the relatives') eyes, and therefore difficult for the relatives to witness.'	Abnormal procedures for relatives Difficult for families to witness	HCP's concern for families' feelings	

Step 8

When you have obtained a revised list, you need to reread the results section of the research paper and make sure that the final categories and subheadings still cover *all the relevant parts* of the results section. Then make any changes you think necessary.

Step 9

Once this has been done for one primary research paper, the same process is carried out for all the included papers. One of Sue's completed data extraction forms is shown in Table 6.10. The process of synthesizing the data extraction forms will be discussed in Chapter 7.

When Sue has extracted her data from one paper, she needs to repeat the process for all her included studies. Sue's data should now be synthesized which means putting it all together or combining it. This is usually carried out by using tables or graphics for quantitative data or presenting them under themes for qualitative data. The ways of doing this will be discussed in Chapter 7.

Table 6.10   One of Sue's completed data extraction forms

Date of data extraction: 19 March 2011
Reviewer: SH
Bibliographical details of study: Goodenough, T. J. and Brysiewicz, P. (2003) 'Witnessed resuscitation: Exploring the attitudes and practices of the emergency staff working in Level I Emergency Departments in the province of KwaZulu-Natal'. *Curationis* 26 (2): 56–63 (supplied by the British Library)
Area: KwaZulu-Natal
Purpose of study: Explore the attitudes and practices of witnessed resuscitation by the staff working in Level I Emergency Departments in the province in the province of KwaZulu-Natal
Study design: Qualitative survey
Setting: Emergency Department

Population:
Sample selection: Purposeful sample of six staff members from two different Level I Emergency Departments. From each of these hospitals the sample consisted of one medical officer, one registered nurse and one registered nurse in charge of the unit. All participants had to be employed in the department for more than six months in order to ensure they had experienced resuscitation procedures. This purposeful selection method was appropriate to the purpose and question as it identified a combination of attitudes from both clinical and managerial staff
Number: Six
Length of experience: Minimum 9 months to 8 years

Exposure: Resuscitation/invasive procedures

(Continued overleaf)

Table 6.10 Continued

Outcome/theme 1
Healthcare professionals' experience of resuscitaton and or invasive procedures

Page	Col.	Line	Data extracted	Sub-themes
60 61	1 1	35–36 1–3	Other concerns stemmed from the insertion of chest drains, defibrillating, putting in tubes, inserting needles and intubation. All of these are invasive procedures that are, 'abnormal in their (the relatives') eyes, and therefore difficult for the relatives to witness.'	Family needs Concern for families' feelings
60	2	26–31	The staff didn't think that the relatives should be present at the resuscitation of their loved one, and they said they would prefer not to be present at the resuscitation of their own family members. 'I totally disagree with allowing family members into the resuscitation room . . .' 'I don't think it's very nice'.	Family needs Concern for families' feelings

Outcome/theme 2
Patient's experience of resuscitaton and/or invasive procedures

Page	Col.	Line	Data extracted	Sub-themes
62	1	1–10	When family members were present the patients, felt loved, supported and less alone. One said, 'It would have been awful to be there alone and have no family there by your side. It would be even worse.' Patients recounted that family members hugged and kissed them, held their hands, and listened to their fears.	Family presence Comfort measures
			One patient undergoing a lumbar puncture said: 'I was scared that it was going to hurt. I didn't want people going in my back. I was afraid. Having him there was so comforting'.	Reassurance from family members
61	1	22–28	Patients described themselves as being 'afraid, hurt, and in pain' during the emergency event.	Family presence
			They related feeling safer and less scared when family members were there.	Comfort measures
			'The injuries were so severe . . . you can deal with a situation like that a lot better if you have the reinforcement of a loved one.' 'I was very scared. I thought I would never have a leg again. It was broken really badly. I thought I might die. I remember waking up and seeing all those doctors. I was like, Where am I? Something is wrong! I looked over and saw my dad and my mother. They were there to help me, to hold my hand, to give me a hug.'	Reassurance from parents' presence

Outcome/theme 3
Family members' experience of resuscitaton and/or invasive procedures

Page	Col.	Line	Data extracted	Sub-themes
59	2	20–21	'I couldn't not have been there, I needed to be with him and I was.' (Fran)	Family needs
59	2	23–28	'I felt useful during the event, I genuinely felt that I was contributing positively and that helps me a lot [pauses]. I can also recall that his eyes were looking at me, as though he knew it was me next to him . . . I was able to keep speaking to him – comforting him – I think!' (Jane)	Feeling conscious of presence Feeling useful during event
59	2	35–39	'John didn't know I was there, of course, he can't remember anything of the event for a good two weeks after . . . And, I didn't think at the time he would know that I was there. I just stood at the foot of his bed – so how could he possibly have known I was there?' (Ann)	Family needs Familiarity and support for patient

---

Practice session 6.3

There are two templates that you can use for your own data extraction. Box 6.5 is for quantitative data extraction and Box 6.6 is for qualitative data extraction.

Box 6.5 Template to use for quantitative generic data extraction

Details of study 1 (bibliographical reference):

Title:

Source:

Purpose of the study:

Reviewer's name: Date:

Study design:

Population:

Sample size:

Criteria of diagnosis:

Any secondary diagnosis:

Exclusion criteria:

Setting:

Intervention:

Comparative intervention:

Outcomes:

Adverse effects:

Box 6.6   Template to use for qualitative generic data extraction

Date of data extraction:

Reviewer:

Bibliographical details of study:

Purpose of study:

Study design:

Setting:

Population:

Sample selection:

Number:

Age:

Education, years:

Ethnicity/race:

Religion:

Relationship of family member:

Primary diagnosis at time of event:

Exposure:

Outcomes: theme 1

Population experiences 1				
Page	Col.	Line	Data extracted	Sub-themes

Outcomes: theme 2

Population experiences 2				
Page	Col.	Line	Data extracted	Sub-themes

Outcomes: theme 3

Population experiences 3				
Page	Col.	Line	Data extracted	Sub-themes

Key points

- The process of selecting studies for inclusion or exclusion in the review consists of two phases.
- The first phase involves sifting through the titles and abstracts of all the articles retrieved from the search, screening them systematically and selecting those that meet the predetermined inclusion criteria.
- The second phase involves reading the full text of each identified article.
- For both phases it is useful to make an appropriate research paper selection form to help you standardize the way you select the articles.
- A quality assessment of your primary papers is one of the key features that sets apart a systematic review from a narrative review.
- To assess the quality of primary articles, a number of assessment tools are available that are easily accessible online or you can use the one included in this chapter.
- It is important to use appropriate checklists or scales for the type of study design to be evaluated.
- Data extraction involves going back to the primary articles and highlighting the relevant information that will answer the research question.
- This involves extracting data related to the population included, the intervention, comparative group and particularly the outcomes (the PICO components).
- To standardize this process and improve the validity of the results, it is crucial to compile a data extraction form.

Summary

This chapter discussed the three main stages involved in working with your primary research papers. The first stage includes ways of selecting appropriate papers to answer your review question. This step is conducted in two parts: select your papers based on the title and abstract according to your predetermined criteria, then repeat this process when reading the full paper. The second stage involves appraising the quality of your primary research papers that you have selected by using standardized quality evaluation frameworks. The third stage is to extract the appropriate qualitative and quantitative data from your research papers. The importance of using a form or framework to standardize and increase the reliability and validity for all stages of the process was clarified by using relevant examples from nursing practice.

7 Synthesizing, summarizing and presenting your findings

Overview

- Issues to consider when synthesizing and summarizing your results
- Tools to use when summarizing and synthesizing your results
- How and where to get started on presenting your results

Issues to consider when synthesizing and summarizing your results

When synthesizing and summarizing your data, there are a number of issues that you need to consider. Popay et al. (2006) state that 'the synthesis, *at a minimum*, is a summary of the current state of knowledge in relation to a particular review question'. (Popay et al. 2006: 6, original emphasis). This is the section where you will attempt to find the answer to your review question. In a quantitative review, if the results are similar enough – for example if the interventions, designs and outcomes are all alike – it may be possible to conduct a statistical procedure, such as a meta-analysis, to combine the results. In a qualitative review the combined results of all the included studies can be synthesized under major themes or sub-themes. This is sometimes called a meta-synthesis or meta-ethnography. It involves a similar approach to the methods of qualitative data analysis used in the primary qualitative studies being synthesized (Noyes et al. 2008).

The Centre for Reviews and Dissemination (University of York) suggests that irrespective of what type of data you have extracted, it is important to first undertake a narrative synthesis of the results of your findings to help you decide what other methods are appropriate. In my opinion this is one of the most exciting parts of the review as it is where you start finding out the answer to your review question. Popay et al. (2006) state:

> 'Narrative synthesis is a form of storytelling . . . bringing together evidence in a way that tells a convincing story of why something needs to be done, or needs to be stopped, or why we have no idea whether a long established policy or practice makes a positive difference is one of the ways in which the gap

between research, policy and practice can start to be bridged. Telling a trustworthy story is at the heart of narrative synthesis.

(Popay et al. 2006: 5)

Popay et al. (2006) have provided some excellent guidance on synthesizing data and have described some specific tools and techniques that can be used when synthesizing your results. They suggest that narrative synthesis may be used in a number of different ways:

- Before undertaking a specialist approach, such as statistical meta-analysis or meta-ethnography.
- Instead of a specialist synthesis approach, because the studies included are insufficiently similar to allow for this.
- When the review question dictates the inclusion of a wide range of research designs [including] qualitative and quantitative designs.

(Popay et al. 2006: 7)

Recapping briefly from Chapter 6, once you have selected your papers, appraised the quality of your papers and extracted the appropriate data, how do you go about synthesizing (or combining) the results obtained from all the primary papers you have included? Some of the key points associated with data extraction can be summarized as follows:

- Are the data sufficiently similar?
- Are there caveats (explanations to prevent misinterpretation) that need to be acknowledged?
- Are there any particular trends or themes?
- Do the data seem to point in one direction or several?

In many disciplines, however, such as nursing and the social sciences, the quantitative studies involved are either significantly different or in many cases involve qualitative studies that require different methods of synthesis. Some reviews may also include studies of different designs (mixed methods). Irrespective of the type of review, there will still need to be some form of summary or synthesis.

Although the primary aim of a review is to answer a clinical question and alter practice, it is important to write up the systematic literature review and publish it so that other nurses can benefit from the findings. Depending on whether the systematic literature review is being conducted for a dissertation or is being written up for journal publication, different results may be presented depending on the submission requirements. Journal articles and the Cochrane Library usually have their own recommendations or criteria for presenting the results.

Tools to use when synthesizing and summarizing your results

There are numerous tools that you can use to summarize, synthesize and present your data. A few of the most common ones are listed below:

- Textual descriptions, which means written words that everyone is familiar with.
- Grouping of similar data, e.g. tabulation (presenting the results in tables).
- Transforming data into a common rubric (name of a particular group or section), for example changing actual numbers from different papers into percentages.
- Charts, which can include histograms, pie-charts and others.
- Translating data either by a thematic or content analysis (Popay et al. 2006).

How and where to get started on presenting your results

This section discusses how to go about summarizing, synthesizing and presenting your results. There are a number of different ways you can do this. The methods for summarizing and synthesizing your data discussed within this book are primarily aimed at the novice reviewer. For more experienced reviewers, the PRISMA (Preferred Reporting Items for Systematic Reviews and Meta-Analyses) document outlines how systematic reviews should be reported for academic journals (www.prisma-statement.org/statement.htm) (Moher et al. 2009).

Essentially the results of everything you have done so far need to be presented, including:

- the results of your search
- the results of the studies selected based on the title and abstract
- the results of the studies selected based on reading the full paper
- a summary of all your included studies
- a summary of all the critiques of the included papers using the appropriate frameworks
- a summary of the data extracted (including a synthesis of the overall results).

All the above are discussed in turn.

Presenting the results of your search

The results of the comprehensive search can be presented either textually or in a table. When writing the search up, it is important to identify all the databases that you have searched and the results you found, so that anyone reading the review can ascertain how comprehensive, transparent and replicable your review is. When presenting the results, it is usual to include the databases searched with the dates included, the date of the search, the number of hits, the number of articles discarded and the number of articles left that need to be reviewed by title and abstract. Results presented in tables also need to be explained fully. Table 7.1 provides an example of how the results of your systematic literature review in nursing could be presented.

Table 7.1   An example of one way of presenting the results of the systematic search

Database with dates	Search date	Number of hits retrieved from the search	Number of articles discarded because of irrelevant titles	Number of articles duplicated from another database	Number of articles to be reviewed by title and abstract
CINAHL (2000–2011)	20/6/12	1569	1456	79	34
MEDLINE (1963–2011)	21/6/12	1847	1346	244	284
EMBASE (1996–2011)	23/6/12	2485	1567	600	318

Practice session 7.1

For your own review question, using the template (Box 7.1), try to fill in the databases you used when searching for your own review question. Write down the dates included, the date of the search, the number of hits, the number of articles discarded and the number of articles remaining that need to be reviewed by title and abstract. As mentioned in Chapter 5, you can now see how important it is to document all your searches! If you don't do this, it will mean that you will need to conduct the search again.

Box 7.1 Template to use for presenting the results of your systematic search

Database with dates	Search date	Number of hits retrieved from search	Number of articles discarded due to irrelevant titles	Number of articles duplicated from another database	Number of articles to be reviewed by title and abstract
CINAHL					
MEDLINE					
EMBASE					

Presenting the results of the studies selected based on the title and abstract

Once the search of a review is conducted, the second step of the systematic literature review is the selection of the primary research studies that meet your inclusion criteria, based on reading the abstracts and titles. Table 7.2 is an example of one way these results could be presented. The first three columns have been filled in to illustrate this point. In column 1 the action is to include the paper as all the criteria have been met. In column 2 the action is to exclude the paper as two of the criteria have not been met. In column 3 the action is to read the full paper before deciding whether to include or exclude the study as it is unclear from reading the abstract whether or not advocacy was included in the primary paper under consideration.

Presenting the results of the studies selected based on reading the full paper

The third step involves presenting the results of the studies included based on reading the full paper and can be presented in a similar format. The final action in this stage is now to include or exclude the paper. Presenting a table like Table 7.2 will enable the reader to know precisely on which selection criteria you based your decision to select your papers. It makes the process of how you conducted your systematic review very clear, transparent and replicable. Remember to include the bibliographic details of the full articles (i.e. the names of the authors, the titles of the articles and the journals they were published in etc.) so the reader can know exactly which papers were included and which were excluded and why.

Table 7.2 An example of one way of presenting the results of the included studies based on reading the title and abstract

Abstract number	1	2	3	4	5
Population Women? Over 18?	✓	✓	✓		
Intervention Advocacy	✓	✓	?		
Comparative group Peer groups or GP treatment?	✓	✗	✓		
Outcomes Women's experiences of interventions?	✓	✗	✓		
Type of study Phenomenological	✓	✓	✓		
*Action Include (read full article) or exclude	Include	Exclude	Read full article		

Practice session 7.2

Now use one of the templates provided to present the inclusion results of the criteria you used for your review. You should already have done this in Chapter 5. Please note that for the first phase of the selection of studies, your actions can be to include, exclude or read the full paper and then make a decision (Box 7.2). For the second phase where you read the full paper, your decision can only be to include or exclude (Box 7.3). Whatever type of review question you have (i.e. either PICO or PEO), the results of the two stages you undertook to select your papers should be presented.

Box 7.2 Template for you to use for presenting the results of the included studies based on reading the title and abstract and using the PICO format

Abstract number	1	2	3	4	5
Population					
Intervention					
Comparative group					
Outcomes					
Type of study					
*Action Include or read full article or exclude					

Box 7.3 Template for you to use for presenting the results of the included studies on reading the full paper and using the PEO format					
Abstract number	*1*	*2*	*3*	*4*	*5*
Population					
Exposure					
Outcomes					
Type of study					
*Action Include or exclude					

Presenting a summary of all your included studies

The fourth step is to provide a summary and present a description of all the primary studies you included within your systematic literature review. Ideally, the details of what is presented should be the same for each study. Tables 7.3 and 7.4 show two examples of how information could be presented in tabular format. In Table 7.3 the first row is filled in as an example of the details that could be included for one study using Mary's case study as an example. In Table 7.4 you can see an example of what one of Sue's paper summaries on witnessed resuscitation could look like. In both versions, the information relating to all components of PICO or PEO need to be provided.

There is another way to present the details for all your included studies and that is simply to write a narrative summary with structured headings (similar to an abstract). If you choose to write it out this way, make sure that you include all the details relating to the population, intervention or exposure and outcomes.

Presenting a summary of all the critiques of your included papers using the appropriate frameworks

In the fifth step, the summary of the results of your critiques can be presented in either tabular or narrative format. When presenting the results of your critiques, it is worth critiquing each study individually and then presenting a shortened version of the answers to all the critique questions for all the studies you included in one comprehensive table. This will likely run into a number of pages. Presenting the overall results of all

Table 7.3   An example of how Mary could describe one study that she included in her review based on all components of the PICO structure

Study	Population	Intervention	Comparative intervention	Outcomes
1. Jones, M. and Smith, L. (2006) Effect of advocacy compared to usual care on women's quality of life. *Clinical Nursing* 20 (1): 56–60	Sample selection: Volunteers recruited from advertisements posted in various community agencies Number: 24 Mean age: 24 years old, range 21–51 years Abusive relationship status: 45% were currently in abusive relationships with no intention of leaving, 35% were trying to leave abusive relationships	60% in individual counselling or a domestic violence support group	40% usual care	Quality of life (QOL) scales Advocacy group pre-intervention QOL values: 30/50 (50 is the average figure for QOL for healthy individuals) Post-intervention QOL values: QOL value 40/50 Usual care group pre-intervention: QOL value 29/50 Post-intervention usual care group: QOL value 30/50 (no difference in QOL post-treatment)

Table 7.4   An example of how Sue could describe one of her qualitative studies using the PEO framework

Paper 2 Full bibliographic reference	O'Brien, J. and Fothergill-Bourbonnais, F. (2004) The experience of trauma resuscitation in the Emergency Department: Themes from seven patients. *Journal of Emergency Nursing* 30 (3): 216–224.
Population	Four men and three women over the age of 18. Four patients were involved in motor vehicle collisions and three suffered falls.
Exposure	Explore the lived experience of patients undergoing resuscitation with and without family presence.
Outcome	Gain an insight of the experiences of patients undergoing resuscitation as shaped by the context of their circumstances.
Results	Four main themes emerged: recollection, confidence in staff, lack of knowledge and experience of being a patient and survival. These main themes consisted of numerous threads: frustration, feeling scared, pain free, kept patients well informed, lack of knowledge and experience of being a patient, tone of voice was calm and soothing, feeling safe, organized and caring, male patients thought family members got in the way, female patients felt that family members presence was a source of comfort and reassurance, feeling important and comforted, going to get out, appreciation for life, positivity and vulnerability.

Practice session 7.3

Select the appropriate template (Boxes 7.4 and 7.5) for your own review question and try to fill in the details of your own included studies.

Box 7.4 Template to use for describing your included studies (PEO format)

Study 1	Population	Intervention	Comparative intervention	Outcomes
Reference				
Population				
Exposure				
Outcome				
Results				

Box 7.5 Template to use for describing your included studies in another way (PICO format)

Study	Population	Intervention	Comparative intervention	Outcomes
1				
2				
3				
4				
5				

your critiques in this way shows that you have appropriately and methodically critiqued the research papers included within your review. Presenting the results of your critiques in this way is helpful when you come to discussing your review (see Chapter 8). Table 7.5 shows a hypothetical example for answering only the first five questions for a paper using Caldwell's critical appraisal framework (Caldwell et al. 2011). Presenting the results in this way is helpful when discussing your results later in your review.

While some critical appraisal frameworks, for example the Caldwell and McMaster frameworks, do not yield a numerical value of the quality of the paper, for the purposes of your own systematic review it is still possible to assign values either for the overall paper quality or for each appraisal question based on your subjective appraisal. A Likert scale can be made up representing the values of 1 through to 5, with 1 representing a paper of very poor overall quality and 5 representing a paper of very good overall quality. Alternatively, it is possible to assign a numerical value to each question and then to add up all the individual scores.

The Caldwell framework has 18 questions. For each question you could have three possible answers (numbers) with an answer of no = 0, partly = 1 and yes = 2. The maximum value that any study could get using the Caldwell framework is 36. At this stage, if you plan only to include studies of good or very good quality in your review, it is important that you state a cut-off point. For example, you could state that any studies achieving fewer than 20 points (out of a total of 36 points) will be excluded from your review. Alternatively you

Table 7.5 An example of how to present the results for the full methodological quality (critical appraisal) of your included studies based on the Caldwell et al. (2011) framework (first five questions only)

Paper	Q1 Does the title reflect the content?	Q2 Are the authors credible?	Q3 Does the abstract summarize the key components?	Q4 Is the rationale undertaking the research clearly outlined?	Q5 Is the literature review comprehensive and up-to-date?
1	Yes, the title includes the population, intervention, comparative intervention and outcomes and accurately reflected the content.	Yes, the authors appear credible. The first author has a doctorate in nursing, which shows her competence to conduct research. The other two authors are both registered nurses.	Yes, the abstract was very comprehensive and structured appropriately with all sections included.	Yes, the rationale for conducting the study was very clear. The authors critiqued all the available literature in the area and very clearly showed the gap in knowledge which they then proceeded to address.	Yes, a comprehensive literature was provided. All the papers mentioned were also appropriately critiqued.

Practice session 7.4

For your own review use one of the templates (Boxes 7.6 and 7.7) based on the Caldwell et al. (2011) framework to critique your papers. You may have already done this when you critiqued each paper individually, so it should now be a simple matter of cutting and pasting the answers from your individual critique to the template. This will allow you to see the results of all the critiques you undertook in a collated format. If your original individual critiques are too long, you could cut and paste only the most important and relevant information. The two templates are similar. The main difference is that the Box 7.6 template does not include a numerical value for each question, whereas the Box 7.7 template does. If you decide to use Box 7.6, you can still rate your paper from 1 (very poor) through to 5 (very good) as discussed above.

Box 7.6 Template to use for presenting your summary of the results of the full methodological quality (critical appraisal) of your included studies based on the Caldwell et al. (2011) framework (first five questions only)

Paper	Q1 Does the title reflect the content?	Q2 Are the authors credible?	Q3 Does the abstract summarize the key components?	Q4 Is the rationale for undertaking the research clearly outlined?	Q5 Is the literature review comprehensive and up-to-date?
1					
2					
3					
4					
5					

Box 7.7 Template to use for presenting your summary of the full methodological quality assessments of your included studies based on the Caldwell et al. (2011) framework, including an overall numerical value

	Questions for qualitative studies based on the Caldwell framework	Paper 1	Paper 2	Paper 3
1	Does the title reflect the content?	Yes 2		
2	Are the authors credible?	Partly 1		
	Background and literature review			
3	Does the abstract summarize the key components?	Yes 2		
4	Is the rationale for undertaking the research clearly outlined?	Yes 2		
5	Is the literature review comprehensive and up-to-date?	Partly 1		
6	Is the aim of the research clearly stated?	No 0		
7	Are all ethical issues identified and addressed?			
	Methods			
8	Is the methodology identified and justified?			
9	Are the philosophical background and study design identified and the rationale for choice of design evident?			
10	Are the major concepts identified?			
11	Is the context of the study outlined?			
12	Is selection of participants described and the sample method identified?			
13	Is the method of data collection auditable?			
	Data analysis			
14	Is the method of data analysis credible and confirmable?			
	Results			
15	Are the results presented in a way that is appropriate and clear?			
16	Are the results transferable?			
	Discussion			
17	Is the discussion comprehensive?			
	Conclusions and implications			
18	Is the conclusion comprehensive?			
	Numerical assessment awarded by author (maximum score is 36 points)	__/36		

could include all the studies (even the poor ones) and then conduct a separate analysis to assess whether the poor studies significantly affected the overall results of your review.

Presenting a summary of the data extracted (including a synthesis of the overall results)

Whatever your review question, in the final step the data you extracted will need to include details related to the population, interventions, comparative interventions (or exposures), and outcomes of all the primary studies you decided to include within your review. All these will now be discussed in turn.

Extracting data relevant to your population group
The way that data extracted from your studies are synthesized and presented depends on the type of data being handled. If you have quantitative data, the usual method is to present them either in tabular format or as a chart. If you have qualitative data, it is usual to present them in themes and sub-themes in a similar way to how the results of a primary qualitative study are presented. With regard to presenting the details related to population groups, ethnicities etc, these data are usually numerical, for example you might say paper 1 had 20 subjects, paper 2 had 40 subjects and so on. If you decide to include the religious affiliation of the populations you are looking at, you may want to consider using something like a pie chart or histogram. Table 7.6, Figure 7.1 and Figure 7.2 are examples of how you could present the number of subjects in each study. Charts and tables can be used to synthesize and present the population numbers in both qualitative and quantitative reviews.

Summarizing, synthesizing and presenting your interventions and comparative interventions
The types of interventions and comparative interventions used in all your included studies could be combined to produce a pie chart or they could be presented in a table. Table 7.7 illustrates how the percentages of participants in the intervention and control interventions could be presented. The pie chart (Figure 7.3) shows an alternative method that could be used.

Summarizing, synthesizing and presenting your outcomes
The summary of the outcomes data extracted depends on the type of data you are handling. If you are synthesizing quantitative data, the usual method is to present the data either in tabular format or as a chart or other alternative graphical format. If they are qualitative data, it is usually easier to present the data through themes and sub-themes. It is important when quoting anything to write down exactly where in the primary paper you got this information from (i.e. state the page, column and line numbers) as you will be referring to this later when you discuss them within the discussion section of your review.

Summarizing, synthesizing and presenting quantitative outcome measures
Outcome measures provide the answer to the research question. As with the population

Table 7.6 Number of participants in all the primary studies included in your review

Article	Number of subjects
Jones (1988)	40
Davies (1992)	60
Smith (2005)	70
Bettany (2008)	80

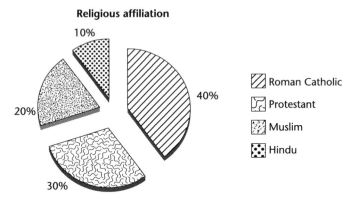

Religious affiliation

Figure 7.1   Religious affiliation for all subjects in all included studies.

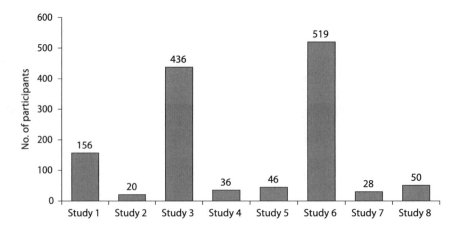

Figure 7.2   Sample size for all included studies.

Table 7.7 Types of interventions

Type of intervention	Number of subjects
Group advocacy	30%
Individual sessions	10%
Both	10%
Usual care	50%

Interventions

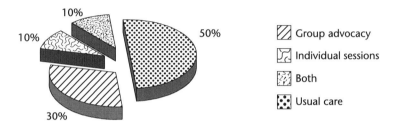

Figure 7.3 Number of subjects in each type of intervention from all included studies.

and intervention, quality of life scores in Mary's case example could be presented in a table or a graph. Table 7.8 and Figure 7.4 show examples of how Mary could present the combined quality of life scores from all her primary studies, both before and after the interventions.

Summarizing, synthesizing and presenting qualitative outcome measures
Qualitative outcome measures are generally synthesized and presented under themes and sub-themes in qualitative primary studies. Presenting qualitative outcomes in systematic literature reviews is no different. Sue could present the outcomes from her qualitative systematic review on witnessed resuscitation in various ways. Sue had three population groups: the patients, the families of the patient and the healthcare professionals. Sue's aim was to appraise their views and perspectives and evaluate any similarities and differences between them which would impact on or change nursing practice. Below are examples of how Sue could synthesize the outcomes from two of her population groups (the patients and the healthcare professionals) under themes and present them in a clear format.

Sue found that three main themes emerged from the patients' experiences of resuscitation and invasive procedures, as follows:

- Theme 1: recollection of the resuscitation and survival instinct
- Theme 2: family presence
- Theme 3: confidence in staff.

One way Sue could present the qualitative outcomes is presented below.

- Theme 1: recollection of the resuscitation and survival instinct
  Seven out of ten studies included in this systematic review identified recollections of fear and frustration by the patient during the resuscitation event, which changed when they saw or heard the voice of a family member. During their family members' presence, the patients felt less alone, and more loved and supported. The extracts below illustrate this:

  > I was very scared. I thought I would never have a leg again. I thought I might die. I remember waking up and seeing all those doctors. I was like, Where am I? Something is wrong! I looked over and saw my dad and my mother. They were there to help me, to hold my hand, to give me a hug.
  >
  > (Eichhorn et al. (2001) page 51, col. 1, lines 22–28)

Table 7.8 Mean quality of life scores before and after advocacy intervention and usual care for all included studies

Mean quality of life scores for each article as measured by the SF-36 scale

	Advocacy group		Usual care group	
	Before	*After*	*Before*	*After*
Jones (2003)	30/50	40/50	29/50	30/50
Davies (2007)	25/50	38/50	24/50	26/50
Smith (1994)	23/50	41/50	23/50	24/50
Bettany (2008)	21/50	44/50	18/50	17/50

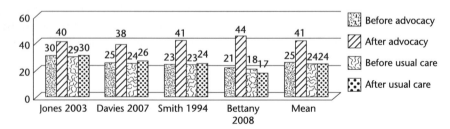

Figure 7.4 Mean quality of life scores before and after advocacy intervention and usual care for all included studies.

> It would have been awful to be there alone and have no family there by your side. I was scared that the lumbar puncture was going to hurt. I was afraid. Having him [my dad] there was so comforting.
>
> (Eichhorn et al. (2001) page 52, col. 1, lines 1–10)

- Theme 2: Family presence
  Five out of ten studies also highlighted the importance of family presence which was a key motivational factor in the patients' belief that they would get out of the A&E department and return to pre-injury life.

> When I knew I was OK – and it's hard to tell why I knew it, but I knew the moment that they started coming around and checking me, I knew that I was going to be okay. I knew it with a surety, especially when I saw my mum and dad were beside me and would be there to help me recover.
>
> (O'Brien and Fothergill-Bourbonnais (2004) page 221, col. 2, lines 17–32)

- Theme 3: confidence in staff
  Six out of ten papers showed that patients had great confidence (trust and faith) in the medical professionals. The extracts below highlight very clearly the strong support and admiration for the healthcare team when the patients sensed and received comfort from the staff and were kept well informed of the procedures that they (patients) were undergoing.

> They warned me there was going to be lots of staff and not to be concerned . . . I felt they were treating me as if I were important.
>
> (O'Brien and Fothergill-Bourbonnais (2004) page 221, col. 1, lines 19–24)

> They always kept me informed . . . that's a very positive reassurance for me that I was part of the team getting me better.
>
> (O'Brien and Fothergill-Bourbonnais (2004) page 220, col. 2, lines 5–11)

For healthcare professionals' experiences of resuscitation and/or invasive procedures, Sue could report the themes and extracts from her data extraction and synthesis of the professionals' perceptions as follows. Sue found that two main themes emerged from healthcare professionals' experiences of resuscitation and invasive procedures.

- Theme 1: judgement call
- Theme 2: threat to comfort zone of healthcare professionals.

Sue could illustrate these two themes in the following way.

- Theme 1: judgement call
  All the primary qualitative papers identified issues relating to staff having to decide whether the situation was viable for family member presence.

> And what is more important, giving the person the right drug or trying to walk around family? I think space is the issue here.
>
> (Timmermans (1997) page 158, col. 1, lines 4–5)

The perceived lack of medical knowledge of the patient's family by the medical staff also contributed to healthcare professionals' decisions as to whether to include or exclude the relatives, as can be seen from the following extract:

> As a layperson, I think it adds insult to injury because there are so many traumatic things that happen therapeutically from a medical perspective but could be perceived as additional trauma.
>
> (Knott and Kee (2005) page 195, col. 1, lines 30–45)

- Theme 2: threat to comfort zone of healthcare professionals
  Another theme which surfaced within all the papers was the challenge that family presence presented to healthcare professionals during the resuscitation or invasive procedure. Family members being present within the resuscitation room made staff question their confidence in their own skills, thus contributing to stressful outcomes for staff as they attempted to do their job. This is clearly seen from the following two extracts:

> OK, let's face it, this is why it makes us uncomfortable. When we are doing resuscitations, we are off . . . it is a mechanical thing. We don't want it to be just a mechanical thing, we want it to be a caring thing and yet we want to remain emotionally aloof so that we can feel that we can function better. We certainly don't want to ever make mistakes in front of a family member. You mix up the drug boxes sometimes. Sometimes you forget to take off a tourniquet . . . Sometimes these things happen. You don't want to ever have a family see you make a mistake in resuscitation. For the family member that is just terrible. You don't want to have something go wrong – an IV gets pulled out accidentally.
>
> (Timmermans (1997) page 158, col. 1, lines 29–40)

> But you do feel like you're on stage, like somebody's watching your performance. But I'm pretty comfortable with my knowledge and skills, so it doesn't really bother me to have somebody there, I just have a heightened awareness . . . You know, we have to show the family that we're doing absolutely everything that we can do, and you start to feel like you're not benefitting the patient, you're actually increasing their suffering.
>
> (Knott and Kee (2005) page 196, col. 2, lines 24–39)

Accompanying these thoughts, another excerpt highlighted concerns that as the healthcare professionals were conducting their job in an effort to sustain life, they may have appeared insensitive in their manner while conducting the resuscitation and this is viewed as being cautious and reflecting on their practice in a judgemental manner, a manner that the relatives may see as not treating their loved one in a caring manner but treating them as if they were 'a person with a condition'.

> 'With every patient you just log on, do your work and that's it. It's not Mr So-and-so. It is a patient, a person with an aortic aneurysm, it's a person with bilateral femoral fractures, it is not a patient with a name and that'. When discussing being present during the resuscitation of their family member, the HCP answered negatively, '. . . you are going to be in the way because you are emotionally involved'.
>
> (Goodenough and Brysiewicz (2003) pages 60–61, cols 2, 1, lines 24–39 and 1–5)

The extracts from both the patients' perspectives and the healthcare professionals' perspectives illustrate that some of their views are similar: both parties are aware of the patients' needs but a number of their perspectives differ significantly. Although the patients feel comforted by the presence of their family members, healthcare professionals are not always comfortable with this and sometimes feel that the relatives get in the way. These similarities and contrasting views will provide very good material for Sue to consider in her discussion section.

Practice session 7.5

If your own review question is qualitative, try writing out the main themes and selecting the most appropriate extracts from the data you extracted in Chapter 6.

Key points

- The synthesis is a summary of the current state of knowledge in relation to a particular review question.
- In a quantitative review, if the results are similar enough, it may be possible to conduct a statistical procedure, such as a meta-analysis, to combine the results.
- In a qualitative review, the combined results of all the included studies can be synthesized under major themes or sub-themes. This is sometimes called a meta-synthesis or meta-ethnography.
- Irrespective of what type of data you have extracted, it is important to always

undertake a narrative synthesis of the results of your findings to help you decide what other methods are appropriate.

- Narrative synthesis is a form of storytelling.
- Narrative synthesis may be used in a number of different ways, including the following:
  o before undertaking a specialist approach such as a statistical meta-analysis or meta-ethnography
  o instead of a specialist synthesis approach because the studies included are insufficiently similar
  o when the review question includes a wide range of different research designs including qualitative and quantitative designs.
- The key points associated with the data extracted to some review questions can be summarized as follows:
  o Are the data sufficiently similar?
  o Are there caveats (explanations to prevent misinterpretation) that need to be acknowledged?
  o Are there any particular trends or themes?
  o Do the data seem to point in one direction or several?
- There are numerous tools that you can use to summarize, synthesize and present your data; some of the more common ones include:
  o textual descriptions
  o grouping of similar data
  o transforming data into a common rubric
  o charts
  o translating data either by a thematic or content analysis.
- The results of everything you did in your review needs to be presented:
  o the results of your search
  o the results of the studies you selected based on the title and abstract
  o the results of your included studies based on reading the full paper
  o a summary of all your included studies
  o a summary of all the papers you critiqued
  o a summary of the data extracted (including a synthesis of the overall results).

Summary

This chapter discussed the issues that you need to consider when summarizing, synthesizing and presenting the results of your quantitative or qualitative systematic literature review in nursing practice. A narrative synthesis needs to be included for whatever type of data you have extracted. This can be done by using a number of different tools to summarize, organize and condense your data. The results of all the methods you have undertaken within your review need to be presented. A key point when summarizing, synthesizing and presenting your results is to make sure that you present everything in a clear, transparent and easy to understand format.

8 Writing up your discussion and completing your review

Overview

- Structuring the discussion of your systematic literature review
- Summarizing your findings in words
- Discussing all the results you presented in the previous section
- Developing and/or discussing the theory on how the intervention or exposure works
- Comparing and contrasting the findings of your study
- Relating the findings back to the objectives set out and the initial area of interest
- Pointing to any methodological shortcomings
- Discussing the ethical aspects of the included studies
- Discussing the findings with respect to practice
- Revealing questions for future research on this topic
- Stating some overall conclusions about the study
- Writing up your systematic literature review
- Academic writing skills: tips on style, grammar and syntax

Structuring the discussion of your systematic literature review

Docherty and Smith (1999) state:

> Structure is the most difficult part of writing, no matter whether you are writing a novel, a play, a poem, a government report, or a scientific paper. If the structure is right then the rest can follow fairly easily, but no amount of clever language can compensate for a weak structure. Structure is important so that readers don't become lost. They should know where they've come from, where they are, and where they are headed. A strong structure also allows readers to know where to look for particular information and makes it more likely that all important information will be included.
>
> (Docherty and Smith 1999: 1224)

Docherty and Smith (1999) suggest that the structure for scientific papers should include a statement of the principal findings, a discussion of the strengths and weaknesses of the study and its strengths and weaknesses in relation to other studies. The meaning of the study findings, as well as implications for practice for clinicians and policy makers, need to be discussed. Finally, the discussion section should conclude by highlighting the importance of addressing unanswered questions and putting forward suggestions for future research. How can you apply these suggestions to writing up the discussion section of your own systematic literature review?

To recap, by now you should have reported the findings from your studies clearly and concisely in the results section. The next step is to discuss your findings fully (as described above). As suggested by Docherty and Smith (1999) and by the Centre for Reviews and Dissemination (2008), start your discussion section with a summary of your major findings (in words, not repeating the figures from the previous section). Discuss your findings through comparing and contrasting your results, and then relate your discussion to the background literature. Ensure that you don't just repeat the results section. The easiest way to do this is to discuss each section in the order that you presented them in the results section. Depending on the type of review (qualitative or quantitative) the theoretical frameworks are usually discussed within the discussion section (mainly for quantitative reviews) while some authors choose to combine the two (i.e. writing up the results and discussion together in the same section; this is conducted more frequently for qualitative reviews). A summary of the key issues that could be included in the discussion section are listed below and then described in detail.

- Summarizing your findings in words
- Discussing all the results you presented in the previous section, in the same order that they were presented, including the following:
  - search results
  - results of the studies selected based on the title and abstract and the results of the included studies based on reading the full paper
  - studies included in your review
  - quality of your included studies in a synthesized format
  - data extracted (including a synthesis of the overall results)
- Developing and/or discussing the theory or theories on how the intervention or exposure works
- Comparing and contrasting the findings of your study
- Relating the findings back to the objectives set out and the initial area of interest
- Pointing to any methodological shortcomings
- Discussing the ethical aspects of the included studies
- Discussing the findings with respect to practice
- Revealing questions for future research on this topic
- Stating some overall conclusions about the study.

Each of the points above will now be discussed using fictitious examples and extracts from the three case studies. A few extracts from the Cochrane Review I participated in are also included (Negrini et al. 2010). Please remember there are a number of ways to do this, each of which will include some or most of the points below. Your discussion needs to be clear, comprehensive and easy for the reader to follow.

Summarizing your findings in words

It is a good idea to start writing your discussion section with a brief summary of the review findings. You could start by discussing the types of research designs that were included. For example, Cheryl in her scoliosis study could say something like this:

> In answer to the review question on the effectiveness of braces for adolescents with idiopathic scoliosis, this review found only six studies that met the strict inclusion criteria. Three of these were randomized controlled studies and three were cohort studies.

Next Cheryl could describe the three randomized controlled trials in more detail and briefly remind the reader the results of these studies:

> One randomized controlled trial (Beaver et al. 2009) compared rigid braces to elastic braces and found low quality evidence in favour of rigid braces. The two randomized controlled trials by Smith et al. (2004) and Thompson et al. (2006) found low quality evidence for the effectiveness of the hard brace versus observation alone. Unfortunately these trials looked at different outcomes and could not, therefore, be combined statistically using a meta-analysis, so the results were synthesized narratively etc.

Cheryl could also discuss any issues that would allow readers to decide if the results were both applicable and relevant to their own practice:

> The studies included only girls, were all written in English and included only the angle of curvature as an outcome. None of the studies looked at outcomes that were important to the patient such as disability, back pain, quality of life and psychological factors.

In other words if the readers of Cheryl's review were nurse practitioners living in Russia where they had mainly male patients and whose main problems were increased pain and a poor quality of life, they would realize that these results would not be applicable to their practice. Cheryl could also qualify her findings by stating that as there were only a small number of studies, the results 'need to be interpreted with caution'.

Discussing all the results you presented in the previous section

All the results presented in the previous section should be discussed in the same order that they were presented.

Discussing the search results

The search results are usually discussed only briefly. You will already have presented details of your comprehensive search in the results section so there is no need to repeat that. What is most important when discussing this section is to highlight any issues of the search process that may have adversely affected your search results and produced biased results. For example, did you search only English-language journals? Was your search truly comprehensive? For example, did you include hand searching of all relevant literature as well as a thorough search for all the grey literature (PhD theses, conference proceedings) relevant to the review question? Did you actually contact any key people in the field to find out whether or not they had further publications in the field? In summary, this is where you highlight what you have or have not done and how this may have introduced any bias in the results of your search. For example, Cheryl could say something like the following:

> A comprehensive search was conducted to retrieve papers that would answer the review question and as a result of reading 90 papers' titles and abstracts, only 20 papers that met the strict inclusion criteria were found. Five papers were then excluded as a result of having read the full papers for the following reasons . . .
> [*here Cheryl would state what the reasons were*]
> and searching papers that were not available electronically was undertaken as well as searching for conference abstracts and PhD dissertations that were available in electronic format. Key people in the field of scoliosis were emailed to ask if they had any unpublished literature that could be included within the review. No documents were obtained. A factor that could have caused bias in paper selection was that the search was restricted only to English-language papers and so will have excluded any primary papers in other languages.

Discussing the results of the studies selected based on the title and abstract and the results of the included studies based on reading the full paper

The subject of this section should only be briefly discussed. Again, any key issues should be highlighted. If you only selected three or four papers out of a total of fifty or more original papers, it is necessary to provide a rationale for this. Maybe your inclusion criteria were too rigid, or perhaps you decided to select a group of participants on which not much had been published. It is important to discuss the papers that were excluded and the reasons for this in more detail so that the reader can understand why you excluded any potentially relevant papers.

Discussing the studies included in your review

In this section you need to provide a discussion of the common (or uncommon) features of all the studies that you included. The easiest way to do this is to go through the summary or description tables of your included studies and then proceed to discuss each part of the PICO or PEO components individually. For example, if you considered the population group of all your included studies, you could discuss how many patients in all were included within the review; were they small or large samples? If the total populations of all your included studies amounted to a very small number, can you really generalize your results? How old were the participants? Did some studies have much older patients while some of them included only very young ones? Could these have had an adverse impact on the outcomes of your results? Were all the studies included conducted within the same type of healthcare setting? If some studies were conducted in a tertiary care setting while others were conducted in care homes, this would let the reader know that the settings were quite diverse. Were all the interventions and comparative interventions exactly the same? If not, how did they differ? Were the outcomes evaluated in all your included studies the same and if not how did this impact on your ability to synthesize the results? All the above are examples of questions that could be discussed depending on your specific review question. Here is an extract from Sue's case study on witnessed resuscitation:

> The seven qualitative studies included within this systematic literature review utilized either grounded theory or descriptive phenomenology. These were chosen for this review as they focused on the lived experience of individuals, aiming to gain an in-depth picture of the populations' feelings and perceptions of the phenomena (Holloway and Wheeler 1996: 15). Beneficial for this review and healthcare research, qualitative research adopts a holistic (person-centred) approach, and in gaining the overall picture of life context, beliefs and values in human environment it becomes a strength of qualitative studies, whereby quantitative methods would be inappropriate as they do not study subjective, humanistic lifestyles (Leininger 1985: 23). As identified by Holloway and Wheeler (2002: 6), quantitative research is useful, although it neglects participants' perspectives within the context of their environment. All the included studies were conducted in a similar setting although the hospitals varied in whether or not they used protocols for witnessed resuscitation. Four out of seven of the studies included the perspectives of the patients and six out of seven the perspectives of the patient, the family and the healthcare professionals.

In Sue's extract, she first provides a rationale for using qualitative research and why this specific methodology is the most appropriate for her review question. Sue clarifies the strengths of qualitative research for evaluating witnessed resuscitation and also explains why quantitative research would not be a suitable methodology. She then goes on to discuss her included papers in more detail.

Discussing the quality of your included studies in a synthesized format

Discussing the quality of your studies is one of the most important aspects of the discussion section and, depending on whether you are planning to write up your results as a report, dissertation or paper, can run into many pages. In Sue's case study, this section will be based on the individual quality appraisals that Sue conducted on each of her studies and which she evaluated earlier on, while conducting her systematic literature review. The key point that Sue needs to remember when writing this section is that the results of all the appraisals of the studies need to be synthesized or combined together to give the reader an *overall summary* of the quality of the papers that were included in the review. This part of the discussion will most likely be one of the longest subsections in the discussion. You will also need to consider whether or not the quality of the included studies affects the outcome of your results. If the methods of a particular study or study were very 'poor', can you still believe the results and apply them to practice? Obviously you cannot. Here is an extract from Sue's systematic literature review on witnessed resuscitation:

> All papers addressed how the studies ensured trustworthiness. Credibility was heightened in papers by Warren et al. (2006) and Crosby (2009) by utilizing member checking, which is considered the most important technique for establishing credibility according to Lincoln and Guba (1985), whereby the researcher returned to the participants to achieve feedback on interpretation (Polit and Beck 2004: 432). Peer debriefing was also carried out in the papers by Andrews et al. (2005), Willowby et al. (2004) and Bell et al. (2010) as the researchers involved peers in reviewing different aspects of the inquiry. Data, investigator, theoretical and methodological triangulation was evident in some of the studies, which strengthens credibility.

Discussing the data extracted (including a synthesis of the overall results)

The data extracted included aspects relating to the PICO elements for quantitative studies and the PEO elements for qualitative studies. Once you have synthesized the extracted data, it is important to discuss these data within the discussion section. Below is an extract from the discussion section from one qualitative outcome from Sue's review, which she discusses under a specific theme.

Theme 1: threat to comfort zone and judgement call

Within this theme, several threads emerged relating to feelings from healthcare professionals that family presence put additional strain on the team conducting the resuscitation process and outlines some choices they had to make when deciding whether the family members should be present, depending on the individuals coping ability. This view was supported by a patient in the study conducted by Eichhorn et al. (2001: 53) who was asked his opinion on how family presence could affect the healthcare environment. He disclosed that it was important that family members understand that they should conduct themselves in an appropriate manner but *'It should be decided on a case-by-case basis – who can handle it and who cannot!'* Knott and Kee (2005: 198) concede that reasons that they do not facilitate family presence is 'insufficient staff', and the potential this event may create psychologically for the family member and lack of space.

Here is an extract concerning the quality of life outcome from a Cochrane review on braces (Negrini et al. 2010):

> ### Quality of life
> Both rigid and elastic braces caused problems, though different kinds of problems. While the rigid brace caused significantly more problems with heat (85% versus 27%), as well as difficulties with donning and doffing, the patients using the elastic braces had difficulties with toileting (Wong 2008). There is low quality evidence from one RCT (N = 43) that a rigid brace is hotter and more difficult to put on and take off than an elastic one, but an elastic one is difficult to manoeuvre during toileting.
>
> (Negrini et al. 2010: 7)

In both the witnessed resuscitation extract and the brace extract, the key issue to be discussed is stated in the first sentence of the paragraph and then the rest of the paragraph goes on to explain what was stated in the first sentence, thus the first sentence is setting the scene for the rest of the paragraph.

Developing and/or discussing the theory on how the intervention or exposure works

In this section it would be helpful, especially if the results of your review are positive or really important (such as witnessed resuscitation), to discuss the theories on how this intervention may work or how policies governing the witnessed resuscitation protocols could be improved or standardized. In Cheryl's review, she could discuss different people's theories as to how hard braces and soft braces work, and what factors may influence whether they work or not, for example compliance (whether or not the patient wears the brace or not). Sue's review on witnessed resuscitation could discuss the importance of witnessed resuscitation to the patients themselves as well as the family, even though the healthcare staff may find it hinders them to have the family around.

Comparing and contrasting the findings of your study

Comparing your findings to the findings of other reviewers is very important. This places the results of your own review within the context of other research and reviews that have already been carried out. Do your review results support the work of others? Do they contradict them? And, if so, why do you believe this is? In the case of the scoliosis brace review, Cheryl could compare her results to other narrative and systematic reviews and discuss the similarities and differences in the population groups, interventions and outcomes, as well as any methodological problems of the included studies and suggest explanations for possible similarities as well as differences. Below is an extract from the Cochrane brace review I participated in (and on which Cheryl's example is based) and this compares how our review was similar to and/or different from other reviews. Suggestions and explanations for these were discussed as seen below:

> An 'evidence-based review' (Dolan 2007) looked at totally different outcomes from those considered here: the 'rate of surgery' (failure of treatment) in braced groups ranged between 1.4% and 41%. This paper was based on retrospective comparative studies, and on retrospective and prospective case series results, all of which were excluded from the current review. Furthermore, only papers in English were considered, while those adding exercises to bracing were excluded. It was not possible to obtain a good uniformity of methods and outcomes among the papers. . . . These problems could be overcome following the SRS criteria for bracing studies (Richards 2005). Moreover, excluding papers that add exercises to bracing should not be done in the future, because according to SOSORT criteria (Negrini 2009), this is a management criterion to increase compliance. In fact, papers including exercises . . . report very low surgery rates, . . . comparable to the best results in the bracing papers reported above.
>
> (Negrini et al. 2010: 9)

Relating the findings back to the objectives set out and the initial area of interest

Relating the findings back to the objectives is an important aspect of the discussion section as the discussion is not a standalone part of the review. Here you need to relate what you found in your results back to your objectives and background section. For example, Cheryl could relate her findings back to her objectives:

> The objective of this study was to evaluate the effectiveness of braces for adolescents with idiopathic scoliosis. The results of this review suggest that there is low evidence for their effectiveness.

Pointing to any methodological shortcomings

Pointing to any methodological shortcomings or flaws in your systematic literature review, and how these may affect the interpretation of the results you have found, is one of the key aspects to include within your discussion. Recommendations on how these shortcomings may be rectified in future studies would also be beneficial. Addressing the limitations of the review enables your readers to judge what parts of the review you could have improved on. Knowing the limitations also allows readers to judge the validity of the results for themselves and how applicable the results may be to their own practice. Here is an example of what Sue could have written for her review on this subject.

Limitations of the systematic review

Due to the primary papers included within this review having numerous methodological shortcomings, the overall outcomes were compromised. The process of reading the full text papers to assess the methodological quality and the data extraction procedure, was conducted alone, which could have given rise to bias.

Discussing the ethical aspects of the included studies

The discussion of the ethical issues within the primary papers that you included within your review is important. If you have evaluated papers that made no mention of any ethical approvals or informed consent of their patients, there is the possibility that the authors conducting the studies might not have considered the issues of informed consent, right to withdrawal etc. As Sue highlights in her dissertation, ethical approval by local ethical committees is considered as an indicator of reliability and validity since it ensures that the study complies with professional, ethical and scientific standards (Tingle and Cribb 2002: 278–285). Here is an excellent discussion on the ethical issues within Sue's systematic literature review:

> As noted by Parahoo (2006: 112), all research studies have individual ethical implications and are sometimes more prominent in one design than another. Importantly, the process of interviewing vulnerable participants – such as those identified within this review – warrants serious ethical consideration. Papers 1, 4 and 5 clearly identify that either verbal or written consent was achieved from the participants and ethical approval obtained from either the Board of Managers within the included hospitals or sponsoring University Review Board. Commendably, paper 4 identified 'beneficence' in providing a 'duty of care' as recommended by the Nursing and Midwifery Council (NMC 2004: 4). The studies all asserted autonomy and confidentiality by issuing a pseudonym to participants and identifying the risks against benefit of exposure prior to the study; they also gave participants the choice to withdraw from the study and access to transcripts. The latter is important in qualitative studies to validate interpretations (Van der Woning 1999: 188).

Discussing the findings with respect to practice

An 'implication for practice' subsection should be included within the discussion section. Improving and enhancing practice is one of the most important reasons for conducting your systematic review. Here is an extract from Sue's review:

Due to the nature of this 'subjective phenomenon', unless having been involved in witnessed resuscitation, it is difficult to understand personal choice. Although the studies delivered strong support for witnessed resuscitation, there were also concerns about negative issues. As recognized in the background literature and throughout this research, cultural diversity affects values, beliefs and behaviours relating to health and illness therefore responses will be subjective (Eichhorn et al. 2001: 54). Through awareness of our own capabilities, we as professional individuals can recognize personal perceptions and biases to accept family choice with respectful autonomy and provide a duty of care (NMC 2004: 4). Through conducting this systematic review it has been identified that further studies should be undertaken to gain knowledge from the patient perspective. One commonality within all the studies except Paper 2 was the recommendation for a protocol especially to deal with the psychosocial requirements of relatives as within Paper 7 attitudes towards family presence changed from negative to positive and further advocates initiating a 'pilot' site so as to provide necessary data to implement change by introducing protocols and education to HCPs and laypersons connected to family presence on a national level in the UK (Hulme 2009).

Revealing questions for future research on this topic

Suggesting areas for future research is a key aspect of any discussion. Include the main points investigated within your review that you would like the reader to remember, highlight what is still not known and include suggestions of the most relevant research that you think should be done to further improve practice in this area.

Stating some overall conclusions about the study

The conclusions of your review should provide a summary of the whole review and restate the key findings. Extracts from first the brace review, and second the witnessed resuscitation review, can be seen below.

Conclusion
Today the only alternative to bracing is the so-called 'wait and see' strategy (i.e. observation and eventual surgery). The scientific evidence is in favour of bracing, but quality is very low ... any future study should look at patient outcomes (not just radiographic outcomes of scoliosis progression) as well as adverse effects, so that balanced conclusions may be generated.

(Negrini et al. 2010: 9)

Conclusion
This systematic review has identified a plethora of views from patients, family members and healthcare practitioners surrounding their individual

experiences of family presence during resuscitation and/or invasive procedures. Each group identified their preferences within themes that were explored
through rich narration, thus giving an overall impression of trustworthiness,
which will contribute to informing practice when utilized with expert clinical
judgement. Derogatory attitudes from fellow family and peers when identifying the research aims and objectives around the phenomenon of 'witnessed
resuscitation' are recalled by the author. This may be through a lack of knowledge and understanding of the topic area and the complexities involved. In
reflection, it would be interesting to find out their opinions of the topic after
reading this review, for it is important that all individuals are given the choice
to be present or not, as in reminiscence, we are all invited to be present at the
birth of our loved ones; therefore should we not be included in their departure
from life? The ability to understand this particular phenomenon can lead to
nursing care that is responsive to the complex experiences of the life world
within the resuscitation room. Supported by protocols such as those developed
by the Emergency Nurses Associations (ENA 2001: Appendix 4), practitioners
can deliver truly holistic care. Until such time, family presence will continue to
be highly debated until protocols are institutionalized to aid the decision-
making process through relevant evidence-based care (Hulme 2009).

Writing up your systematic literature review

The final step in conducting your systematic literature review is writing it up to a high
standard. Depending on why you are conducting your systematic literature review, you
may need to write up a dissertation, a journal article, a hospital report or a paper for a
commissioning body. Irrespective of where you are planning to write up your review, it
is important to take as much care in writing it up as in conducting the review. The
report should include all aspects of the systematic review process including the
background, objectives, inclusion and exclusion criteria, methods of selecting and
appraising your papers, extracting relevant data, the results section, the discussion and
conclusions.

As discussed earlier, by the time you have written up the plan or protocol of your
review, you should already have the first five major sections written up, albeit in the
future tense. Once you have completed your review, having the plan written up makes
completing the review much easier as you will not be starting from scratch.

You will need to go back to your plan and update the background section (there
may have been more papers or relevant reviews published by this time). You should
already have your objectives, inclusion and exclusion criteria, methods for selecting
and appraising your papers and data extracting written up, although it will be worth
checking them over to ensure you did what you said you would do in your original
plan. You should now have only two major sections to write up – the results and the
discussion sections, including the conclusion.

It is important to ensure that your report is written up clearly and with great attention to detail, similar to the writing up of a scientific paper. It needs to contain enough

detail so other nurses or researchers can replicate your review just by reading through it. The literature suggests that poor quality reporting of primary papers affects readers' ability to interpret the results. Many reports suggest that reviews (as well as intervention papers) often omit crucial details about the interventions or methods of the review, thereby limiting the ability of clinicians and readers of the systematic literature review to evaluate the findings and limit clinicians' ability to implement the findings in practice (Cochrane Effective Practice and Organisation of Care 2011). Ideally, similar to the writing up of your discussion section, it is best to structure the presentation of your review. Box 8.1 suggests how to present all the sections in the write up of your report.

Box 8.1 Suggested structure of a systematic literature review

Title

Acknowledgements

Abstract

Contents page

Abbreviations or glossary (if relevant)

Structured abstract

- Background
- Objectives
- Search strategy
- Study selection
- Study appraisal
- Data extraction and synthesis
- Results
- Discussion
- Conclusions

Main text

1   Background
2   Review question(s)
3   Objectives
4   Search strategy
5   Study selection
6   Study appraisal
7   Data extraction and synthesis
8   Results
9   Discussion
10 References
11 Conclusions
12 Appendices

Academic writing skills: tips on style, grammar and syntax

Many people assume that any literate person can write a research proposal. This is not quite accurate. It is one thing to write a letter or an email to a friend when you go on holiday but quite another matter when it comes to writing in an academic style. Writing is a complex skill to master and the only way that most people improve their writing skills is through practice, perseverance and dedication.

When writing up your report it is important to make sure your writing style is in the correct tense. Before completing your report, try to check the spelling, grammar and syntax. Reading a systematic literature review that is full of spelling errors is off-putting and gives the impression that the review was done carelessly and without attention to detail. The following are some tips to help you write up your review and help with your academic writing:

- If you are stuck and have writer's block, try using mind-mapping exercises or brainstorming with colleagues.
- If possible, try to structure your work in advance.
- Know what you want to convey before trying to write it.
- Every sentence should contain one idea only.
- Each sentence should follow logically from the one before. A well-written text is a chain of ideas.
- When you write a new paragraph, introduce the main idea of the paragraph in the first line of the paragraph and then go on to elaborate and give related examples in the rest of the paragraph.
- Try to link your paragraphs so that the text reads logically. If you put ten different ideas in ten different paragraphs and do not connect them in any way, the reader may think you are talking about many disconnected ideas.
- You could try to link the paragraph above to the one below by writing something related to the next paragraph in the last sentence of the paragraph before.
- While writing keep your reader's needs in mind. This means providing a verbal 'map' of your document so that your reader knows what to expect, and placing verbal 'signposts' in your text to explain what is coming next.

Key points

- Plan and structure the discussion section of your review.
- Start your discussion with a summary of your findings in words.
- Ensure that you discuss all the results you presented in the results section:
  - Discuss the results of the studies you selected based on the title and abstract and based on reading the full paper.
  - Discuss your included studies in terms of PICO or PEO.
  - Discuss the quality of your included studies in a synthesized format.
  - Provide a detailed discussion of the data extracted.

- Develop and/or discuss any theory or theories as to how the intervention (or exposure) works.
- Compare and contrast the findings of your study.
- Relate the findings back to the objectives set out and the initial area of interest.
- Make recommendations on how these shortcomings may be rectified in future.
- Discuss the findings with respect to practice and/or policy.
- Discuss the ethical aspects of the included studies.
- Reveal questions for future research on this topic.
- Finish your discussion by stating some overall conclusions about the study.
- Provide overall conclusions about your review.
- Write up your systematic review to a high standard (this is a fundamental part of the systematic literature review process).
- Take as much care in writing up the review as in conducting the review.
- Ensure that you include all aspects of the systematic review process in the:
  - background
  - objectives
  - inclusion and exclusion criteria
  - methods of selecting your papers
  - appraisal of your papers
  - extraction of relevant data
  - results section
  - discussion section
  - conclusions.
- Finally, take great care over the presentation of your review: check your spelling grammar and syntax.

Summary

This chapter discussed ways of structuring the discussion section of your systematic literature review. Extracts from case studies and a completed systematic review were presented. Suggestions for writing up your review report were described together with tips for improving academic writing skills.

9 Sharing, disseminating and using systematic reviews to inform and improve nursing practice

Rob McSherry, Professor of Nursing and Practice Development

Overview

- The importance of sharing and disseminating
- Defining sharing and disseminating
- Methods of sharing and disseminating
- Models and frameworks supporting or hindering the implementation of evidence-based nursing
- Enablers and inhibitors to sharing and disseminating
- Implementing the findings of systematic reviews in practice

The importance of sharing and disseminating

The previous chapters have defined and detailed the steps you will have taken as you undertook a systematic review of your own. This chapter describes the importance of sharing and disseminating the findings.

Systematic reviews, as indicated in Chapter 1, encourage evidence-based nursing. To practise evidence-based nursing successfully, Thompson et al. (2004) suggest several factors that influence decisions about patient care:

- an understanding of the importance of practice being based on the most appropriate evidence
- access to and the ability to use research findings
- the ability to evaluate research and the ability to implement research findings in their own practice.

Put simply, to achieve evidence-based nursing, you need to be evidence informed, which involves:

> providing clinically effective patient care and being able to justify the proce-
> dures used, the care plan devised or the services provided by reference to

authoritative evidence. It is the making of decisions about the care of individual patients and families, on the basis of the best available evidence.

(McSherry et al. 2002: 3)

The challenge for some academic researchers or nurses who have undertaken a systematic review is in devising a strategy for the sharing and dissemination of their research findings. Bradley et al. (2010) highlight the difficulties faced by frontline nurses and midwives in resolving and rising to the challenges associated with accessing, reviewing and translating research in support of their decision-making and actions in practice. The importance of sharing and disseminating the findings from research and systematic reviews is crucial in the quest to inform and improve nursing and midwifery practice.

'It is unreasonable to expect people such as clinicians, policy makers, or patients who want reliable information about the effects of healthcare to unearth the relevant evidence from reports of original research' (Chalmers 2006: 156). Hence researchers need to incorporate strategies and action plans for the sharing and dissemination of their results within the original research proposal or systematic review.

Lavis et al. (2005: 35) suggest 'that systematic reviews of research evidence constitute a more appropriate source of research evidence for decision-making than the latest or most heavily publicized research study'. This is because the dissemination of the results and findings from original research and systematic reviews can contribute to the following:

- adding new knowledge to the field
- evaluating specific nursing interventions and practices
- focusing on improving the quality of nursing and midwifery care and interventions and associated patient outcomes
- helping services to adopt and implement innovation
- supporting the practising of evidence-based nursing.

The failure to share and disseminate the findings from research and systematic reviews could impact on the following:

- building an evidence-base for nursing and midwifery
- informing healthcare management and policy
- establishing impact and outcomes of care
- offering equity through knowledge exchange and translation
- advancing innovation and change.

Despite all the evidence highlighting the importance of sharing and disseminating the findings from original research and systematic reviews to improve the quality of nursing care, interventions and outcomes, why do nurses continue to struggle to utilize evidence in support of their decision-making in practice? This may be occurring because nurses need to:

- be informed by evidence and research findings (incorporating findings from systematic reviews)
- have the critical appraisal skills to evaluate evidence and skills to implement the findings
- have the time to access evidence and be supported by managers, and professional colleagues to do so.

Defining sharing and disseminating

Generally 'sharing' is defined as 'to receive, use, in common with others' and 'dissemination' is defined as 'to scatter far and wide' (Collins 1987). Collectively sharing and disseminating could be regarded as the 'process of implementing the findings of research' by which target groups become aware of, receive and utilize information (Freemantle and Watt 1994: 133). The Centre for Reviews and Dissemination (2008) defines dissemination as the:

> planned and active process that seeks to ensure that those who need to know about a piece of research get to know about it and can make sense of the findings. As such it involves more than making research accessible through traditional mediums of academic journals and conference presentation.
>
> (Centre for Reviews and Dissemination 2008: 85)

Lord Rosenheim, President of the Royal College of Physicians, addressed the World Health Organization (WHO) in 1968, and claimed that: 'If, for the next 20 years, no further research were to be carried out . . . the application of what is already known, of what has already been discovered, would result in widespread improvement in world health' (quoted in Bradley et al. 2010: 20).

The concerns of Lord Rosenheim signalled caution regarding the amount of research being carried out worldwide, without effective implementation. More recently, the House of Lords Select Committee on Science and Technology voiced concern at the delay in translating research findings into practice (Parliamentary Business 2010). The failure to translate research with proven benefits into action could result in improvements to patient care being delayed, primarily through difficulties with effective dissemination. Furthermore, research in these areas may be being undertaken that is unnecessary, raising concerns about the ethics of including patients in studies which are not required. Despite concerns being raised in the 1960s, the dissemination of research findings still remains a challenge for research and development departments within health and social organizations and universities. Indeed, this challenge is recognized globally (Bradley et al. 2010). What are the best ways to share and disseminate your results, findings and recommendations from a systematic review?

Ensuring effective communication of the results and findings, according to the Centre for Reviews and Dissemination (2008), requires careful consideration of several key attributes (Box 9.1).

Box 9.1 Characteristics and attributes for effective sharing and dissemination

- *The characteristic of the research message:* associated with identifying key messages from the findings and how and why these may influence knowledge and attitudes.
- *The setting in which the message is received:* targeting the specific presentation of the findings, the language used, format, structure, type and audience appeal.
- *The characteristic of the target audience:* directed at targeting and prioritizing the main audience(s). The relevance and receptivity of the findings should be determined and shared accordingly.
- *The source of the research message:* refers to the attractiveness, importance, trustworthiness and credibility of the findings to be shared and disseminated.
- *The presentation of the research message:* harnessing and engaging with a variety of sources in devising a strategy for communicating and exposing the message to the target audience.
- *The communications channel(s) used:* dependent on making the relevant information and messages accessible, interpretable, actionable to appropriate target audiences.

Source: Centre for Reviews and Dissemination (2008)

McSherry and Simmons (2002) offer several similar principles that encapsulate the key characteristics and attributes to guide the sharing and dissemination of your results or findings (Table 9.1).

According to Table 9.1, devising a strategy and action plan for the sharing, dissemination and implementation of your results or findings is primarily dependent on effective communication (Centre for Reviews and Dissemination 2008). An effective strategy and action plan for the sharing and disseminating of the findings from a systematic review should focus on achieving the following:

- Ensuring that the essential message(s) from the findings reach the specific target audience(s) associated with the area of practice reviewed.
- Providing the findings in a format or style that is both accessible and relevant to frontline nurses and midwives.

Methods of sharing and disseminating

Focusing on 'knowledge transfer' is defined by the Nursing Health Service Research Unit (NHSRU 2011) as:

> A continuum of processes and activities that bring researchers and decision-makers together from the stage of idea generation to implementing evidence-based initiatives. Researchers and decision-makers influence each other's shared and separate mandates to generate timely and relevant evidence and make it available and accessible. In turn, stakeholders assess the utility of the

Table 9.1   Principles and rationale for effective sharing and dissemination

Principle	Rationale
Communication	Effective communication through verbal and non-verbal means is essential in sharing the findings and key messages from your systematic review.
	Ensuring your results and key messages are successfully shared and disseminated requires the following:
	• *Sufficient time:* for preparing and presenting the findings.
	• *Accuracy and clarification*: ensuring a clear, concise and accurate summary of the review's findings and recommendations.
	• *Acknowledgement of limitation:* identifying any key issues or challenges associated with the review.
	• *Avoidance of the use of jargon:* keeping the messages and information simple and easy to understand.
	• *Seeking and acting upon feedback*: encouraging individuals to critique the review and respond accordingly.
	• A *strategy and action plan:* devising a simple strategy and action plan for sharing and disseminating your findings is essential in communicating your key message(s).
Presentation	Focusing on what is the best way to get over the key message(s) from the findings of your systematic review or research requires time, energy and commitment to see things through.
	Whatever the format, style or type of presentation, it requires the findings to be detailed in a clear, concise, logical and organized way, whether this is oral, written, and/or a combination of both.
	Ensure you avoid overuse of jargon and communicate your message effectively.
Target audience	Considering who you are going to feed back the findings to: are they individuals or organizations?
	Contacting and communicating with the relevant parties before forwarding information and keeping records of to who, when and how you shared your findings is good for monitoring progress and the effectiveness of your sharing and dissemination.
Resources	Sharing and disseminating your findings costs money!
	Avoiding disappointment at the end of the review process is critical.
	Ensure that costing for the sharing and dissemination of your findings is built into the original proposal.
	Liaising with relevant stakeholders about funding and supporting the sharing and disseminating of the findings is important.
	Accessing internal organizational support such as the research and development, audit and/or service improvement and/or practice development departments, is a resourceful way to ensure you have support to share and disseminate your findings.
Facilitation	Accessing individuals both internally and externally who may have the knowledge and skills to support you with sharing and disseminating your key messages is a useful way of getting your findings recognized.

evidence for their own settings and use it for the purpose of informing and advancing their decision-making in the areas of policy, practice, or planning.

(NHSRU 2011: 1)

Based on the NHSRU (2011) definition of knowledge transfer, it is imperative to identify some practical initiatives for sharing and disseminating your findings. According to the Centre for Reviews and Dissemination (2008), these may include paper and electronic publishing, email alerting services and mass media campaigns. McSherry and Simmons (2002: 130) suggest: 'In order to avoid disappointment after completing a review that you want to share with colleagues, it is essential to consider prior to the review the potential financial implications and sources of funding'. Some practical tips are offered in Box 9.2.

Box 9.2 Practical tips for successfully sharing and disseminating your review findings

- *Consulting*
  - ○ Approach leaders and managers prior to undertaking your review to seek approval and sources of support for both resources and finance to aid with sharing and dissemination.
  - ○ Contact other departments, for example communications, medical photography, clinical audit, research and development, service improvement and transformation, for support with devising a strategy and action plan for sharing and disseminating the findings.
- *Utilizing*
  - ○ Engage with your professional colleagues and embrace the experience within your local and external organizations in seeking and confirming ways for effective sharing and dissemination.
- *Negotiating*
  - ○ Arrange access to information technology, computer technology and other potential relevant computer software with relevant departments to help with the sharing and dissemination of your findings.
  - ○ Negotiate taking time out from your work to ensure that you undertake your review effectively and to avoid the pitfalls of having insufficient time and support.
- *Collaborating*
  - ○ Contact local universities, research and development faculties and departments to seek academic and expert support.

Source: adapted from McSherry and Simmons (2002: 130)

Effective sharing and disseminating of your systematic review and/or research findings is dependent on ensuring you incorporate the importance of knowledge transfer and dissemination within the original proposal. Sharing and disseminating of the review or research findings according to Becheikh et al. (2011) is a complex process requiring a robust strategy that focuses on four major areas:

- dissemination of the findings
- reception of users of the findings
- adoption of the findings
- utilization of the information in practice that can be supported and hindered by models and frameworks.

Models and frameworks supporting or hindering the implementation of evidence-based nursing

Rycroft-Malone and Bucknall (2010) suggest that since 2000, several international models or frameworks have been developed, explored and evaluated; these are transferable across different health and social care settings, supporting the implementation of evidence-based practice as part of innovation and change. In his PhD thesis 'Developing, exploring and refining a modified whole systems based model of evidence-informed nursing,' McSherry (2007) offers some examples of models and frameworks supporting getting evidence into practice. This section is based on McSherry (2007).

Kitson et al. (1998) stressed the importance of exploring new ways of making it easier to get evidence into practice. This perhaps explains the rise in the number of frameworks and models dedicated to facilitating such a cause, some of which are highlighted by Rycroft-Malone and Bucknall (2010) and McSherry (2007). To ensure that results, findings and recommendations from your systematic review become a part of the evidence base, it is imperative for you to know and understand some of the models and frameworks that exist to aid you with this process.

Practice session 9.1

Can you identify any models or frameworks that support the implementation of evidence into practice?

Read on and compare your notes with the remainder of the section.

You may have found Practice session 9.1 challenging and wonder 'Why is this?' It is not a common practice to offer the various models or frameworks that are available to support getting evidence into practice as part of the teaching and education of research forming part of nurse education and training (Bradley et al. 2010). So what are models and frameworks and how do they support getting evidence into practice?

What are models and frameworks?

For most nurses using any of the frameworks or models, the challenge is in differentiating one from the other. Wright (1990) describes a framework as a structure to hold together, or to support, something – a basic structure or system. A model is regarded as a representation of an existing or planned object, a standard of excellence to be imitated

(Aggleton and Chalmers 1986). By applying Wright's (1990) and Aggleton and Chalmers' (1986) work to this situation, it is evident that frameworks and models are different, yet equally important, in providing a means to an end; that is, encouraging nurses and midwives to use evidence in support of practice. Some models and frameworks, rather than encouraging engagement, actually discourage engagement, because of their complex design and terms used. *Frameworks* appear to focus on promoting specific element(s) of evidence-based nursing; these include encouraging research utilization (Mohide and King 2003), or enhancing decision-making (Thompson 1999). *Models* are built up from a collection of evidence-based ideas or concepts, highlighted by frameworks, such as the impact of organizational culture on evidence-based nursing (Kitson et al. 1998) and the importance of providing support (Sanares and Heliker 2002), each having formal systems and mechanisms to produce change. Despite these differences, such frameworks or models generally aim to organize nurses' thinking about evidence-based nursing, so that they are able to transfer that thinking into practice, with order and effectiveness.

What models and frameworks are available?

Numerous frameworks and models have been developed to facilitate putting evidence into practice. These comprise both frameworks (Funk et al. 1991; Mohide and King 2003; Newhouse et al. 2005) and models (Stetler 1994; Kitson et al. 1996; Rosswurm and Larrabee 1999; Hogan and Logan 2004; Rycroft-Malone et al. 2004). Some of the various models and frameworks are detailed in Table 9.2 (at the end of the chapter), which attempts to offer the following information below:

- some of the various frameworks and models that exist
- their purpose
- key strengths and weaknesses
- what element(s) of evidence-based nursing they are associated with
- how they contribute to getting evidence into nursing.

Table 9.2 reveals that existing frameworks and models vary from simple to complex. They are designed to target factors that support or hinder individuals or organizations using evidence in practice. These include isolating and resolving the barriers that affect research utilization and application in practice (Funk et al. 1991) and ensuring that nurses have sufficient resources, such as time to access the internet and time to read research articles.

How do models and frameworks support getting evidence into practice?

Some major features influence the utilization of evidence in practice. These include the person and the process. Stetler (1994) places the responsibility for engaging with and using evidence in practice with the individual professional or person, but evidence-based nursing cannot be undertaken in isolation. Nurses require organizational encouragement to develop, so that they can equip themselves with the knowledge, skills and confidence to use evidence in practice. Evidence-based nursing will only happen if the organizational culture and working environment are conducive to change; that is, by being supportive and facilitative in empowering nurses to innovate and learn new knowledge and approaches to service delivery, improvement and evaluation.

The process of getting evidence into practice requires the creation of an organizational culture and working environment that proactively, not reactively, respond to innovation and new ways of working. Kitson et al. (1996) and Rycroft-Malone et al. (2004) argue that the creation of an organizational culture and working environment, conducive to getting evidence into practice, needs to focus on enhancing development of three core elements – evidence, context and facilitation:

- *Evidence* places strong emphasis on the individual and organization being able to distinguish types of evidence, ways to access it, interpret it and apply it in practice.
- *Context* refers to the unique working environment of the organization and how this is influenced by structural, economic, societal, political and historical events and positions.
- *Facilitation* pertains to how facilitators, such as practice developers, have a key role to play in helping individuals and teams to understand what they need to change and how they need to change it, in order to apply evidence to practice.

Enablers and inhibitors to sharing and disseminating

Many enabling and inhibiting factors influence the sharing and dissemination of the findings. These factors are highly complex and challenging. Empirical studies by Kitson et al. (1996, 1998), Rycroft-Malone et al. (2004), Upton and Upton (2005) and Van Achterberg et al. (2006) concur that getting evidence into practice through the sharing and dissemination of research findings from systematic reviews and/or original research is challenging because of four major factors:

- individual attitudes
- organizational and cultural influences
- education and training
- terminological confusion.

Individual attitudes

Attitudes do influence the way that nurses view and use evidence. Banning's (2005) qualitative study, associated with the various evidence-based approaches, concluded that nurses displayed a positive regard for evidence, but lacked confidence in articulating the terms. Banning's (2005) study shows that since the mid-1980s, attitudes towards research and evidence-based nursing have remained unchanged. The challenge lies in establishing why nurses view evidence-based nursing and its associated processes positively, despite not knowing what these mean. A study by Clarke et al. (2005) that evaluated the utilization of evidence-based guidelines on pressure-ulcer treatment concluded that 'although a responsibility of each nurse, evidence-based practice requires supportive professional practice environments that include leadership and commitment from nurse managers' (Clarke et al. 2005: 578).

Taking the findings of Clarke et al. (2005) into account, could nurses within the UK (Banning 2005; Upton and Upton 2005) be agreeing with the principles of evidence-based nursing because of a growing fear of not keeping up with healthcare trends and expectations from employers, professional regulating bodies and the public? Carnwell's (2000) study confirmed this idea, by suggesting that the real problem of getting evidence into practice is that nurses find it difficult to differentiate research from evidence. Retsas's (2000) study extends this thought, by suggesting that a lack of accessibility of research findings anticipated outcomes of using research, and that a lack of organizational support and support from others are the major inhibitors. The significance of the studies by Retsas (2000) and Carnwell (2000) lies in highlighting the necessity to develop a shared responsibility and appropriate culture, between the individual and organization, for getting evidence into practice.

Organizational and cultural influences

The view that organizational cultures and working environments influence evidence-based nursing could be attributed to the work of Funk et al. (1991) through their development of the Barriers to Research Utilization Rating Scale. Funk et al. (1991) showed that the major barriers included a perceived lack of organizational and management support to engage with research, a lack of time to read journals, and research studies often being reported in an unreadable and inaccessible format. Since the publication of the original study by Funk et al. (1991), some international studies by Oranta et al. (2002) and Retsas (2000) have used the Funk et al. (1991) barriers scale. These studies have reported similar findings to Funk et al. (1991), enhancing the validity and reliability of the measurement instrument. Despite its proven success in reporting lack of organizational and managerial support for engaging with research. Rycroft-Malone et al. (2004) believe that the major barriers to getting evidence into practice are culturally based, in the way that individuals and organizations respond in facilitating and supporting innovation and change.

Udod and Care's (2004) work, which utilized the Funk et al. (1991) questionnaire, illustrated how workload, skill-mix issues and shortages of nurses in the clinical setting frequently leave nurses too exhausted to engage with research or campaign for change. This is a concern, highlighted by Caine and Kenrick (1997), when investigating the role of clinical directors in facilitating evidence-based practice. Similarly, Nagy et al. (2001) argue for the importance of managerial and organizational support and resources for getting evidence into practice. Both Nagy et al. (2001) and Rycroft-Malone et al. (2004) air a degree of caution that enhancing human and financial support may not necessarily improve the chances of getting evidence into practice. Nagy et al. (2001) suggest several other complex factors to be taken into account. These include nurses' belief in the value of research, knowledge of research language and having sufficient time.

Perhaps this is why Udod and Care (2004) argue that individual and organizational responsibility for getting evidence into practice transcends the organizational culture and working environment to the educational and clinical settings.

Education and training

Walsh (1996) argues that evidence-based nursing is dependent on the communication of a new language, alien to the majority of nurses, so misunderstanding and confusion are inevitable. Walsh (1996) suggests that communication plays a pivotal role in practising evidence-based nursing, because it is a multidimensional term, made up of a series of key systems and processes that need to collect and transfer information. These include a nurse's knowledge of evidence-based nursing (Fulbrook 2003; Melnyk 2004) and an appreciation of research awareness (Cullen and Titler 2004), in order to inform their decision-making ability (Thompson et al. 2004). The effectiveness of the communication processes, within and between these various elements, is critical. Brown's (1995) use of communication theory, to illustrate that it is not the message sent that matters, but the message received, is an important point in the quest for evidence-based nursing. McSherry et al. (2002) argue that this is because nurses need to be informed of the various elements and how these work, collectively, to help the transference of evidence. Ineffective communication arises when nurses distance themselves from engaging with the terms, because of the complex jargon and language used (French 1999). Furthermore, the various elements of evidence-based nursing have been portrayed as single entities, rather than a collective whole, making it almost impossible to understand and interact with in practice. To resolve these practices, Pickering and Thompson (2003) argue that academics and researchers need to focus on the way they present and communicate information. If they write and teach in a way that supports other academics or teachers, it is not surprising that some nurses do not understand or use research in practice. This is because they receive a message that research is not for them, but for academics. The issues over language and communication between clinicians, academics, researchers and managers might be summarized as 'culture clash'.

McCormack et al. (2002) suggest that cultural differences between the various institutions are creating the barriers to evidence-based nursing. In the past, nursing in the NHS undervalued research, by favouring rituals and tradition, creating two subcultures of researchers and clinicians, each having different aims, opinions and values. To redress these imbalances, Dawes et al. (2005) argue that schools of health need to develop educational and training programmes on evidence-based approaches relevant to the needs of the NHS organizations and of nurses themselves. Dawes et al. (2005) believe that the use of a clinical practice-oriented and multiprofessional approach and delivery is required, showing where the research evidence is and how this impacts on the patient's outcome of care. One example of presenting research that is meaningful is the use of in-depth case studies, and McSherry and Proctor-Childs (2001) suggest that the use of case studies could alleviate some nurses' concerns about research and implications for practice. This is because of its holistic and multiprofessional approach, in presenting the full picture, case, context and evidence-base, by drawing upon the expertise and experiences of the professionals. The growing evidence for evidence-based nursing to be taught more efficiently and effectively to students must be done in a way that engages rather than disengages. Confusions and misunderstandings with terminology, therefore, must be explored and eradicated from the nursing curriculum and service setting.

Terminological confusion

Irrespective of the emergence and formal recognition of evidence-based nursing within the evidence-based movement, nurses continue to struggle with understanding and engaging with the terms. This is because a plethora of information has emerged, which is trying to decipher what evidence-based nursing is not, or what it ought to be. As a consequence, Jennings and Loan (2001) argue that a discourse has emerged, embracing the various evidence-based nursing permutations, leading to growing confusion, misunderstanding, distortion and, finally, misconceptions of the term. Zeitz and McCutcheon (2003) contend that the advancement of evidence-based nursing is the solution to achieving best practice by arguing that 'basic nursing practices remain unquestioned, are based on tradition instead of evidence, are regulated, do not require clinical decision-making and that the patient is merely a recipient rather than an integral part of practice' (Zeitz and McCutcheon 2003: 272).

Taking Zeitz and McCutcheon's (2003) evidence into account, the misconceptions could be attributable to the fact that nurses are actively encouraged to acquire the knowledge and understanding of evidence-based nursing, irrespective of knowing the relative merits and demerits of engaging with the term. The reality of achieving evidence-based nursing is fraught with difficulty, because of the complex systems and processes required to operate this at an individual, organizational and clinical level. A possible way forward in resolving these issues, in the future, is to confirm the universal elements required for evidence-based nursing to occur.

Implementing the findings of systematic reviews in practice

The sharing and disseminating of the results and findings from a systematic review or original research should not be regarded as an adjunct, but integral to the review and research process. The devising of strategies and action plans for the sharing, dissemination and implementation of the results and findings should be incorporated within the primary stages of the review proposal. Devising ways to effectively communicate results and findings is imperative along with enlisting the support of existing models and frameworks available to translate and facilitate getting evidence into practice. Ensuring nurses are informed of, and able to utilize, evidence as part of their decision-making process is critical in ensuring evidence-based nursing. Evidence-based nursing is not optional but forms a major part of a nurses and midwives professional code of practice, contract of employment, continuing professional development and lifelong learning. By sharing and disseminating results in a manner that is accessible, relevant, reliable and consistent you are contributing to ensuring that quality nursing care becomes an expectation for all patients, carers and users in the future.

Key points

- The challenge for some academic researchers and nurses who have undertaken a systematic review is in devising a strategy for the sharing and dissemination of their research findings.
- The importance of sharing and disseminating the findings from research and systematic reviews is crucial in the quest to inform and improve nursing practice.
- Despite concerns being raised in the 1960s, the dissemination of research findings still remains a challenge for research and development departments within health and social organizations and universities.
- Devising a strategy and action plan for the sharing, dissemination and implementation of your results and findings is primarily dependent on effective communication.
- Effective sharing and dissemination of your systematic review or research findings is dependent on ensuring you incorporate the importance of knowledge transfer and dissemination within the original proposal.
- To ensure the results, findings and recommendations from your systematic review become a part of the evidence base, it is imperative for you to know and understand some of the models and frameworks that exist to aid you with this process.
- Many enabling and inhibiting factors influence the sharing and disseminating of the findings.
- The sharing and disseminating of the results and findings from a systematic review or original research should not be regarded as an adjunct, but integral to the review and research process.

Summary

This chapter discussed the importance of sharing and disseminating the findings from systematic reviews in informing and improving nursing practice. The chapter defined the terms sharing and disseminating and described their relevance to spreading the findings from systematic reviews. Practical tips and ways of sharing and disseminating systematic reviews were illustrated, along with some of the models and frameworks to enable and support innovation and change in organizations providing nursing practice. The chapter outlined the enabling and inhibiting factors associated with the implementation of the findings of systematic reviews in practice.

Appendix

Table 9.2 Models and frameworks promoting evidence-based practice in year order

Author(s)	Year and location	Title	Journal details	Description	Purpose	Key contributions	Strengths	Weaknesses	Evidence-based precept
Stetler, C.B.	1994 USA.	Stetler Model of Research Utilization.	*Journal of Nurse Administration* 28 (7): 45–53.	Presents the newly devised Stetler Model of Research Utilization.	To present a model to encourage nurses in practice to utilize research in practice.	The development of a practitioner-based model for research utilization. Placed the responsibility for research utilization firmly with the nurse.	The development of the Stetler Model of Research Utilization. Simple to follow. Contains five components centred on encouraging the practitioner to engage with research.	Lack of attention to organizational and cultural influences on getting evidence into practice.	Research awareness.

| Kitson, A., Ahmed, L.B., Harvey, G., Seers, K. and Thompson, D. | 1996 UK. | From research to practice: One organizational model for promoting research-based practice. | *Journal of Advanced Nursing* 23 (3): 430–440. | Presents a framework used to integrate research, development and practice within a healthcare organization. | To explore the impact of integrating deductive and inductive approaches to project development. | The development of an integrated framework for research and practice. | Highlighted the importance of adopting an integrated approach to organizational development. Provides framework for effective organizational change by focusing on evidence, context and facilitation. | Involves complex methods making replication of the work less attractive. It may be regarded as unrealistic to expect staff working in practice to successfully work towards using an integrated approach when considering organizational improvement and change. | Research awareness. Research appreciation and utilization. Facilitation. |

(*Continued overleaf*)

Table 9.2 Continued

Author(s)	Year and location	Title	Journal details	Description	Purpose	Key contributions	Strengths	Weaknesses	Evidence-based precept
Rosswurm, M.A. and Larrabee, J.H.	1999 USA.	A model for change to evidence-based practice.	*Image – Journal of Nursing Scholarship* 31(4): 317–322.	Presents a model based on theoretical and research literature related to evidence-based practice, research utilization, standardized language and change theory.	To describe a model that guides nurses through a systematic process for the change to evidence-based practice.	The development of a six stepped model to guide practitioners through the entire process of changing to evidence-based protocols.	The application of the model to develop an evidence-based protocol for hospitalized patients with acute confusion. Reaffirms the key components of the evidence-based process.	Emphasis on developing research awareness skills to the jeopardy of other precepts associated with getting evidence into practice.	Evidence-based process. Research awareness.

| Rycroft-Malone, J., Kitson, A., Harvey, G., McCormack, B., Seers, K., Titchen, A., and Estabrooks, C. | 2002 | UK. | Ingredients for change: Revisiting a conceptual framework. | *Qualty and Safety in Healthcare* 11(2): 174–180. | Theoretical developments to PARIHS Framework. | To gain greater clarity of the three key elements that affect change and getting evidence into practice by undertaking a concept analysis. Enabled the team to scrutinize the PARIHS framework and sub-elements by reviewing research and work to date. | Provided greater detail to validate the model and how the three elements • evidence • context • facilitation integrate to influence and structure change. | Provided confirmatory data to challenge and enhance the comprehensive nature of the framework. | Reinforces the need for simplification of the framework. Further work to explain what constitutes the sub-elements. | Conditions affecting evidence-based nursing. Support. |

(*Continued overleaf*)

Table 9.2 Continued

Author(s)	Year and location	Title	Journal details	Description	Purpose	Key contributions	Strengths	Weaknesses	Evidence-based precept
Mohide, E.A. and King, B.	2003 Canada.	Building a foundation for evidence-based practice: Experiences in a tertiary hospital.	*Evidence-Based Nursing* 6 (4): 100–103.	Depicts how the merger of four different healthcare organizations, cultures and facilities was achieved through the development of an evidence-based practice model for nursing.	To depict the processes involved in developing an evidence-based practice model for a new emerging organization.	Highlights the importance evidence-based practice plays in supporting successful mergers of healthcare facilities.	Highlights the challenges and opportunities of healthcare mergers. Reinforces the importance of organizational structures and cultures in promoting evidence-based nursing. Provides a working model for developing evidence-based nursing practice.	Limited acknowledgement of the challenges and difficulties associated with the process.	Conditions affecting evidence-based nursing. Research awareness. Resources.

Hogan, D. and Logan, J.	2004 Canada.	The Ottawa Model of Research Use: A guide to clinical innovation in the NICU.	*Clinical Nurse Specialist* 18 (5): 255–261.	The establishment of the Ottawa Model of Research Use (OMRU) to guide clinical innovation in a neonatal intensive care unit.	To address the issues surrounding involving family during the transportation of neonates.	The development of a family-centred approach to transporting neonates, using the newly-devised Family Assessment Tool to guide practice.	Depicts the systems and processes involved in devising and achieving a family-centred approach to neonatal transportation. Presents the Family Assessment Tool, a flow chart involving a series of Likert scale responses to a series of questions surrounding • practice environment • potential adopters • evidence-based innovation.	Specialist centred making transferability of the innovation difficult to achieve within the wider context of evidence-based nursing.	Conditions affecting evidence-based nursing. Decision-making. Research awareness.

(Continued overleaf)

Table 9.2 Continued

Author(s)	Year and location	Title	Journal details	Description	Purpose	Key contributions	Strengths	Weaknesses	Evidence-based precept
Newhouse, R., Dearholt, S., Poe, S., Pugh, L.C. and White, K.M.	2005 Dearholt, UK.	Evidence-based practice: A practical approach to implementation.	*Journal of Nursing Administration* 35 (1): 35–40.	Highlights the development of a model to support nurses to become more systematic and critical in implementing and evaluating guidelines and pathways.	Encourages nurses to engage with the evidence-based processes.	Provides a practical model using an evidence-based educational package and mentorship programme to encourage nurses to become more confident and competent with the evidence-based process.	Combination of educational and clinical-based methods. Simplistic and easy to follow.	Having sufficient educated mentors to support staff in practice. Overcoming the barriers of balancing workload and time.	Professional accountability. Decision-making. Conditions affecting evidence-based nursing.

References

Aggleton, P. and Chalmers, H. (1986) *Nursing Models and the Nursing Process*. London: Macmillan Education.

Alderson, P. and Green, S. (2002) *Cochrane Collaboration Open Learning Material for Reviewers*. Available at www.cochrane-net.org/openlearning (accessed 6 July 2010); http://jpubhealth.oxfordjournals.org/cgi/content/abstract/27/4/388

Armstrong, R., Jackson, N., Doyle, J., Waters, E. and Howes, F. (2005) It's in your hands: The value of handsearching in conducting systematic reviews of public health interventions. *Journal of Public Health* 27 (4): 388–391. Available at http://jpubhealth.oxfordjournals.org/cgi/content/abstract/27/4/388 (accessed 13 November 2011).

Asher, M., Min, L.S., Burton, D. and Manna, B. (2003) The reliability and concurrent validity of the Scoliosis Research Society-22 patient questionnaire for idiopathic scoliosis. *Spine* 28 (1): 63–69.

Bailey, D.M. (1997) *Research for the Health Professional: A Practical Guide*, 2nd edn. Philadelphia, PA: F.A. Davis.

Banning, M. (2005) Conceptions of evidence, evidence-based medicine, evidence-based practice and their use in nursing: independent nurse prescribers' views. *Journal of Clinical Nursing*, 14 (4): 411–417.

Becheikh, N., Ziam, S., Idrissi, O., Castonguay, Y. and Landry, R. (2011) How to improve knowledge transfer strategies and practices in education? Answers from a systematic literature review. *Research in Higher Education* 7: 1–21.

Blaikie, N. (2007) *Approaches to Social Enquiry*, 2nd edn. Cambridge: Polity Press.

Bradley, E., McSherry, W. and McSherry, R. (2010) Disseminating research: How joint NHS and university posts can support this process. *Nursing Times* 106 (46): 20–23.

Brown, G.D. (1995) Understanding barriers to basing nursing practice upon research: A communication model approach. *Journal of Advanced Nursing* 21 (1): 154–157.

Bruce, N., Pope, D. and Stanistreet, D. (2008) *Quantitative Methods for Health Research: A Practical Interactive Guide to Epidemiology and Statistics*. London: Wiley.

Burnard, P. (1991) A method of analysing interview transcripts in qualitative research. *Nurse Education Today* 11 (6): 461–466.

Caine, C. and Kenrick, M. (1997) The role of clinical directorate managers in facilitating evidence-based practice: A report of an exploratory study. *Journal of Nursing Management* 5 (3): 157–165.

Caldwell, K., Henshaw, L. and Taylor, G. (2005) Developing a framework for critiquing health research. *Journal of Health, Social and Environmental Issues* 6 (1): 45–54.

Caldwell, K., Henshaw, L. and Taylor, G. (2011) Developing a framework for critiquing health research: An early evaluation. *Nurse Education Today* 31 (8): e1–7.

Carnwell, R. (2000) Essential differences between research and evidence-based practice. *Nurse Researcher* 8 (2): 55–68.

Centre for Evidence-Based Medicine (CEBM) Centre for Evidence-Based Medicine, Oxford, UK. Available at www.cebm.net (accessed 18 September 2009).

Centre for Reviews and Dissemination (CRD) (2008) *Systematic Reviews: CRD's Guidance for Undertaking Reviews in Health Care.* Available at www.york.ac.uk/inst/crd/systematic_reviews_book.htm (accessed 29 June 2010).

Chalmers, I. (2006) *The Cochrane Collaboration: Preparing, Maintaining, and Disseminating Systematic Reviews of the Effects of Health Care.* Available at http://onlinelibrary.wiley.com/doi/10.1111/j.1749-6632.1993.tb26345.x/pdf (accessed 28 February 2011).

Clarke, H.F., Bradley, C., Whytock, S., Handfield, S., van der Wal, R. and Gundry, S. (2005) Pressure ulcers: Implementation of evidence-based nursing practice. *Journal of Advanced Nursing* 49 (6): 578–590.

Cochrane Collaboration (2002) *Cochrane Collaboration Open Learning Material for Reviewers: Version 1.1.* Available at www.cochrane-net.org/openlearning (accessed 29 June 2010).

Cochrane Collaboration (2009) *Cochrane Handbook for Systematic Reviews of Interventions.* Available at www.cochrane-handbook.org (accessed 29 June 2010).

Cochrane Effective Practice and Organisation of Care (2011) *Cochrane Effective Practice and Organization of Care (EPOC) Group.* Available at http://epoc.cochrane.org (accessed 7 December 2011).

Collins, W. (1987) *Collins Universal English Dictionary.* Glasgow: Readers Union.

Craig, J. and Smyth, R.L. (2007) *The Evidence-Based Practice Manual for Nurses,* 2nd edn. London: Churchill Livingstone.

Cullen, L. and Titler, M.G. (2004) Promoting evidence-based practice: an internship for staff nurses. *Worldviews on Evidence-Based Nursing* 1 (4): 215–223.

Dawes, M., Summerskill, W., Glasziou, P., Cartabellotta, A., Martin, J., Hopayian, K., Porzsolt, F., Burls, A. and Osbourne, J. (2005) Sicily statements on evidence-based practice. *BMC (BioMed Central) Medical Education* 5 (1): 1–7.

DiCenso, A., Cullum, N. and Ciliska, D. (1998) Implementing evidence-based nursing: Some misconceptions. *Evidence-Based Nursing* 1 (2): 38–40.

Dickersin, K., Chan, S., Chalmers, T.C., Sacks, H.S. and Smith, H. (2002) Publication bias and clinical trials. *Controlled Clinical Trials* 8: 243–353. Available at www.ncbi.nlm.nih.gov/pubmed/3442991?dopt=Abstract (accessed 30 January 2012).

Docherty, M. and Smith, R. (1999) The case for structuring the discussion of scientific papers. *British Medical Journal* 318: 1224.

Douglas, R.M., Hemilä, H., Chalker, E. and Treacy, B. (2004) Vitamin C for preventing and treating the common cold. *Cochrane Database of Systematic Reviews.* Issue 3.

Egger, M., Zellweger-Zähner, T., Schneider, M., Junker, C., Lengeler, G. and Antes, G. (1997) Language bias in randomized controlled trials published in English and German. *The Lancet* 350 (9074): 326–329.

Field, P.A. and Morse, J.M. (1985) *Nursing Research: The Application of Qualitative Approaches.* London: Chapman and Hall.

Flemming, K. (1998) Asking answerable questions. *Evidence-Based Nursing* 1: 36–37.

Freemantle, N. and Watt, I. (1994) Dissemination: Implementing the findings of research. *Health Libraries Review* 11 (2): 133–137.

French, P. (1999) The development of evidence-based nursing. *Journal of Advanced Nursing* 29 (1): 72–78.

Fulbrook, P. (2003) The nature of evidence to inform critical care nursing practice. Unpublished PhD thesis, Bournemouth University, UK.

Funk, S.G., Champagne, M.T., Wiese, R.A. and Torquist, E.M. (1991) Barriers to using research findings in practice: The clinician's perspective. *Applied Nursing Research* 4 (2): 90–95.

Glaser, B.G. and Strauss, A. (1967) *Discovery of Grounded Theory. Strategies for Qualitative Research.* Mill Valley, CA: Sociology Press.

Glasziou, P., Irwig, L., Bain, C. and Colditz, G. (2001) *Systematic Reviews in Health Care: A Practical Guide.* Cambridge: Cambridge University Press.

Goodenough, T.J. and Brysiewicz, P. (2003) Witnessed resuscitation – Exploring the attitudes and practices of the emergency staff working in Level 1 Emergency Departments in the province of KwaZulu-Natal. *Curationis* 26 (2): 56–63.

Greene, M. (1997) The lived world, literature and education. In D. Vandenberg (ed.) *Phenomenology and Educational Discourse.* Johannesburg: Heinemann.

Hemmingway, P. and Brereton, N. (2009) *What is a Systematic Review?* Available at www.whatisseries.co.uk/whatis/pdfs (accessed 30 January 2012).

Higgins, J.P.T. and Deeks, J. (2009) *Cochrane Handbook for Systematic Reviews of Interventions.* Available at www.cochrane-handbook.org (accessed 6 July 2010).

Hogan, D. and Logan, J. (2004) The Ottawa Model of Research Use: A guide to clinical innovation in the NICU. *Clinical Nurse Specialist* 18 (5): 255–261.

Jadad, A. (1998) *Randomized Controlled Trials: A User's Guide.* London: BMJ Books.

Jenkins, S., Price, C.J. and Straker, L. (1998) *The Researching Therapist: A Practical Guide to Planning, Performing and Communicating Research.* Edinburgh: Churchill Livingstone.

Jennings, B.M. and Loan, L.A. (2001) Misconceptions among nurses about evidence-based practice. *Journal of Nursing Scholarship* 33 (2): 121–127.

Khan, K.S., Kunz, R., Kleijnen, J. and Antes, G. (2003) *Systematic Reviews to Support Evidence-Based Medicine: How to Review and Apply Findings of Healthcare Research.* London: Royal Society of Medicine Press.

Kitson, A.L., Ahmed, L.B., Harvey, G., Seers, K. and Thompson, D. (1996) From research to practice: One organizational model for promoting research-based practice. *Journal of Advanced Nursing* 23 (3): 430–440.

Kitson, A.L., Harvey, G. and McCormack, B. (1998) Enabling the implementation of evidence-based practice: A conceptual model. *Quality in Health Care* 7: 149–158.

Knott, A. and Kee, C.C. (2005) Nurses' beliefs about family presence during resuscitation. *Applied Nursing Research* 18: 192–198.

Lahlafi, A. (2007) Conducting a literature review: How to carry out bibliographical database searches. *British Journal of Cardiac Nursing* 2 (12): 566–569.

Lai, S.M., Asher, M. and Burton, D. (2006) Estimating SRS-22 quality of life measures with SF-36: Application in idiopathic scoliosis. *Spine* 31 (4): 473–478.

Lavis, J., Davies, H., Oxman, A., Denis, J.L., Goldend-Biddle, K. and Ferlie, E. (2005) Towards systematic reviews that inform healthcare management and policy making. *Journal of Health Service Research and Policy* 1 (1): 35–48.

McCormack, B., Kitson, A., Harvey, G., Rycroft-Malone, J., Titchen, A. and Seers, K. (2002) Getting evidence into practice: the meaning of 'context'. *Journal of Advanced Nursing* 38 (1): 94–104.

McCormack, H.M., Horne, D.J. and Sheather, S. (1988) Clinical applications of visual analogue scales: A critical review. *Psychological Medicine* 18 (4): 1007–1019.

McSherry, R. (2007) Developing, exploring and refining a modified whole systems based model of evidence-informed nursing. Unpublished PhD thesis, Teesside University, Middlesbrough.

McSherry, R. and Proctor-Childs, T. (2001) Promoting evidence-based practice through an integrated model of care: Patient case studies as a teaching method. *Nurse Education in Practice* 1: 19–26.

McSherry, R. and Simmons, M. (2002) The importance of research dissemination and the barriers to implementation. In R. McSherry, M. Simmons and P. Abbott (eds) (2002) *Evidence-Informed Nursing: A Guide for Clinical Nurses*. London: Routledge.

McSherry, R., Simmons, M. and Abbott, P. (eds) (2002) *Evidence-Informed Nursing: A Guide for Clinical Nurses*. London: Routledge.

Melnyk, B.M. (2004) Editorial. *Worldviews on Evidence-based Nursing* 1 (2): 83.

Moher, D., Liberati, A., Tetzlaff, J., Altman, D.G. and the PRISMA Group (2009) Preferred Reporting Items for Systematic reviews and Meta-Analyses: The PRISMA Statement. *British Medical Journal* BMJ 2009;339:bmj.b2535. Available at www.bmj.com/content/339/bmj.b2535.full?view=long&pmid=19622551 (accessed 30 January 2012).

Mohide, E.A. and King, B. (2003) Building a foundation for evidence-based practice: Experiences in a tertiary hospital. *Evidence-Based Nursing* 6 (4): 100–103.

Nagy, S., Lumby, J., McKinley, S. and Macfarlane, C. (2001) Nurses' beliefs about the conditions that hinder or support evidence-based nursing. *International Journal of Nursing Practice* 7 (5): 314–321.

Negrini, S., Minozzi, S., Bettany-Saltikov, J., Zaina, F., Chockalingam, N., Grivas, T.B., Kotwicki, T., Maruyama, T., Romano, M. and Vasiliadis, E.S. (2010) *Braces for Idiopathic Scoliosis in Adolescents*. Cochrane Review. Available at http://onlinelibrary.wiley.com/doi/10.1002/14651858.CD006850.pub2/pdf (accessed 20 November 2011).

Newhouse, R., Dearholt, S., Poe, S., Pugh, L.C. and White, K.M. (2005) Evidence-based practice: A practical approach to implementation. *Journal of Nursing Administration* 35 (1): 35–40.

NMC (2004) *The NMC code of professional conduct: standards for conduct, performance and ethics.* London: NMC.

Noyes, J., Popay, J., Pearson, A., Hannes, K. and Booth, A. (2008): Qualitative research and Cochrane reviews. In J.P.T. Higgins and S. Green (eds) *Cochrane Handbook for Systematic Reviews of Interventions. Version 5.0.1* (updated September 2008). Cochrane Collaboration. Available at www.cochrane-handbook.org (accessed 20 November 2011).

Nursing Health Service Research Unit (NHSRU) (2011) *Knowledge Transfer*. Available at www.nhsru.com/knowledge-transfer (accessed 17 October 2011).

O'Brien, J.A. and Fothergill-Bourbonnais, F. (2004) The experience of trauma resuscitation in the emergency department: Themes from seven patients. *Journal of Emergency Nursing* 30 (3): 216–224.

Oranta, O., Routasalo, P. and Hupli, M. (2002) Barriers to and facilitators of research utilization among Finnish registered nurses. *Journal of Clinical Nursing* 11 (2): 205–213.

Parliamentary Business (2010) Bioengineering – Science and Technology Committee 'Translating Research'. Available at www.publications.parliament.uk/pa/cm200910/cmselect/cmsctech/220/22006.htm (accessed 17 October 2011).

Pauling, L. (1974) Are recommended daily allowances for vitamin C adequate? *Proceedings of the National Academy of Sciences of the United States of America* 71 (11): 4442–4446.

Petticrew, M. and Roberts, H. (2006) *Systematic Reviews in the Social Sciences: A Practical Guide.* Oxford: Blackwell.

Pickering, S. and Thompson, J. (eds) (2003) *Clinical Governance and Best Value: Meeting the Modernisation Agenda.* London: Churchill Livingstone.

Popay, J., Roberts, H., Sowden, A., Petticrew, M., Arai, L., Rodgers, M. and Britten, N. (2006) *Guidance on the Conduct of Narrative Synthesis in Systematic Reviews.* Version 1. Lancaster University, UK.

Retsas, A. (2000) Barriers to using research evidence in nursing practice. *Journal of Advanced Nursing* 31 (3): 599–606.

Rooda, L.A. (1994) Effects of mind mapping on student achievement in a nursing research course. *Nurse Educator* 19 (6): 25–27.

Rosswurm, M.A. and Larrabee, J.H. (1999) A model for change to evidence-based practice. *Image – Journal of Nursing Scholarship* 31 (4): 317–322.

Rycroft-Malone, J. and Bucknall, T. (eds) (2010) *Models and Frameworks for Implementing Evidence-Based Practice: Linking Evidence to Action (Evidence-Based Nursing).* Oxford: Wiley-Blackwell.

Rycroft-Malone, J., Kitson, A., Harvey, G., McCormack, B., Seers, K., Titchen, A. and Estabrooks, C. (2002) Ingredients for change: Revisiting a conceptual framework. *Quality and Safety in Healthcare* 11 (2): 174–180.

Rycroft-Malone, J., Seers, K., Titchen, A., Harvey, G., Kitson, A. and McCormack, B. (2004) What counts as evidence in evidence-based practice? *Journal of Advanced Nursing* 47 (10): 81–90.

Sackett, D.L., Richardson, W.S., Rosenberg, W. and Haynes, R.B. (1997) *Evidence-Based Medicine: How to Practice and Teach EBM.* New York: Churchill Livingston.

Sanares, D. and Heliker, D. (2002) Implementation of an evidence-based nursing practice model: Disciplined clinical inquiry. *Journal of Nurses Staff Development* 18 (5): 233–238.

Schulz, K.F. and Grimes, D.A. (2002) Case-control studies: Research in reverse. *The Lancet* 359 (9304): 431–434.

Scoliosis Research Society (SRS) (2006) Glossary. Scoliosis Research Society. Available at www.srs.org/patients/glossary.php (accessed 5 December 2011).

Spradley, J.P. (1979) *The Ethnographic Interview.* New York: Holt, Rinehart and Winston.

Stetler, C.B. (1994) Stetler Model of Research Utilization. *Journal of Nurse Administration* 28 (7): 45–53.

Thompson, C. (1999) A conceptual treadmill: The need for 'middle ground' in clinical decision making theory in nursing. *Journal of Advanced Nursing* 30 (5): 1222–1229.

Thompson, C., Cullum, N., McCaughan, D., Sheldon, T. and Raynor, P. (2004) Nurses, information use, and clinical decision making: The real world potential for evidence-based decisions in nursing. *Evidence-Based Nursing* 7 (3): 68–72.

Timmermans, S. (1997) High touch in high tech: The presence of relatives and friends during resuscitative efforts. *Scholarly Inquiry for Nursing Practice* 11 (2): 154–168.

Timmins, F. and McCabe, C. (2005) How to conduct an effective literature search. *Nursing Standard* 20 (11): 41–47.

Tingle, J. and Cribb, A. (eds) (2002) *Nursing Law and Ethics*, 2nd edn. Oxford: Blackwell.

Torgerson, C. (2003) *Systematic Reviews*. London: Continuum.

Udod, S.A. and Care, D.W. (2004) Setting the climate for evidence-based nursing practice: What is the leader's role? *Nursing Leadership* 17 (4): 64–75.

Upton, D. and Upton, P. (2005) Nurses' attitudes to evidence-based practice: Impact of a national policy. *British Journal of Nursing* 14 (5): 284–288.

Van Achterberg, T., Holleman, G., Van De Ven, M., Grypdonck, M.H.F., Eliens, A. and Van Vliet, M. (2006) Promoting evidence-based practice: The roles and activities of professional nurses' associations. *Journal of Advanced Nursing* 53 (5): 605–612.

Walsh, M. (1996) Perceptions of barriers to implementing research. *Nursing Standard* 11 (19): 34–37.

Weiss, H.R., Reichel, D., Schanz, J. and Zimmermann-Gudd, S. (2006) Deformity related stress in adolescents with AIS. *Studies in Health Technology and Informatics* 123: 347–351.

Wright, S.G. (1990) *Building and Using a Model of Nursing*. London: Edward Arnold.

Zeitz, K. and McCutcheon, H. (2003) Evidence-based practice: To be or not to be, this is the question! *International Journal of Nursing Practice* 9 (5): 272–279.

Index

DOING A LITERATURE REVIEW IN HEALTH AND SOCIAL CARE
A Practical Guide
Second Edition

Helen Aveyard

9780335238859 (Paperback)
2010

eBook also available

This bestselling book is a step-by-step guide to doing a literature review in health and social care. It is vital reading for all those undertaking their undergraduate or postgraduate dissertation or any research module which involves a literature review.

The new edition has been fully updated and provides a practical guide to the different types of literature that you may be encountered when undertaking a literature review.

Key features:

- Includes examples of commonly occurring real life scenarios encountered by students
- Provides advice on how to follow a clearly defined search strategy
- Details a wide range of critical appraisal tools that can be utilised

www.openup.co.uk

OPEN UNIVERSITY PRESS
McGraw · Hill Education